Praise for the Designers and *Fine Foliage*

"Garden lovers, you now have the secret for creating the landscapes of your dreams – the ones you see in magazines and wonder: *'How do those designers DO THAT?'* Christina and Karen show you how to look beyond the flowers and introduce you to the real stars of the horticultural world – LEAVES!"

— **Ivette Soler,** *Garden designer and author of* The Edible Front Yard

"Step into the pages of this wonderful book – an extraordinary collection of foliage combinations for all seasons, in shade or sun. If you take even a small part of what *Fine Foliage* is placing in front of you, your life will be enriched."

— **Nicholas Staddon,** *Director of New Plant Introductions, Monrovia Growers*

"In her garden designs and containers, Christina combines plants in ways that are simple yet aesthetically delightful and innovative. Christina's work has made such an impression on me, whenever I see a leaf with great variegation, texture or veining, I think of her."

— **Debra Lee Baldwin,** *author of three books on using succulent plants in garden design*

"I only wish Karen Chapman lived close to me so that she could be my personal gardening coach. Rarely do you find a garden designer who not only can create dazzling plant combinations but also is able to teach the rest of us how to do the same."

— **Danielle Sherry,** *Senior Editor, Fine Gardening*

"Christina Salwitz is a design professional who successfully translates design principles into stunning plantings. Her ability to combine color and form creates beautiful garden tapestries."

— **Patty Dunning,** *Horticulture magazine content leader*

"Christina's container designs are bold and arresting. She is fearless when in comes to combining color, texture and shape in a small area."

— **Susan Cohan, APLD,** *Co-founder and Editor of Leaf magazine*

"Karen Chapman's container designs prove that the eye of a talented designer can inspire a whole new appreciation for the amazing variety of colors and textures to be found in the beautiful but often overlooked world of foliage."

— **James Augustus Baggett,** *Editor, Country Gardens*

"Christina Salwitz shares her considerable design talents with fellow gardeners. Those looking to take their garden creativity beyond the usual blooms and into the realm of foliage composition will be well rewarded."

— **Eric Liskey,** *Deputy Editor, Gardens & Outdoor Living, Better Homes and Gardens*

"Karen and Christina are a powerhouse of horticulture knowledge and magical design perspectives. *Fine Foliage* is full of gorgeous images and stellar ideas that will make even those who don't garden drool with horticultural lust."

— **Danielle Ernest,** *Proven Winners*

"In Karen Chapman's universe, tropicals and hardies, woodies and herbaceous plants, classy perennials and common vegetables get along like one big happy family. Tasteful landscapes and gorgeous containers help tie everything together, and Karen's wonderful sense of whimsy keeps it all fun."

— **Jim McCausland,** *garden writer*

"Container designer Christina Salwitz artfully employs color, contrast, texture, pattern, size, shape and form to magical effect…with stunning combinations of leaf and twig, easily achieved by any gardener looking to up the wattage in their garden."

— **Janet Endsley,** *Seminar & Social Media Manager, Northwest Flower & Garden Show*

"The beautiful photographs, diverse and unique combinations and easy-to-follow recipes in *Fine Foliage* are sure to increase both new and experienced gardeners' enjoyment and success."

— **Melinda Myers,** *gardening expert, TV/radio host, author and columnist*

fine FOLIAGE

Elegant Plant Combinations for Garden and Container

fine FOLIAGE

Elegant Plant Combinations for Garden and Container

KAREN CHAPMAN | CHRISTINA SALWITZ

st. lynn's press

PITTSBURGH

FINE FOLIAGE
Elegant Plant Combinations for Garden and Container

ISBN-13: 978-0-9855622-2-9

Library Of Congress Control Number: 2012940815
Cip Information Available Upon Request

First Edition, 2013

ST. LYNN'S PRESS . POB 18680 . PITTSBURGH, PA 15236
412.466.0790 . www.stlynnspress.com

Book design – Holly Rosborough, St. Lynn's Press
Editor – Catherine Dees

All images ©Ashley DeLatour, except for the following:
Images on pages 14-15, 34-35, 78-79, 80-81, 96-97, 100-101,
104-105, 118-119, 122-123, 124-125 ©Karen Chapman
Images on pages 6-7, 24-25, 48-49 ©Christina Salwitz

Printed in Canada
on certified FSC recycled paper using soy-based inks

This title and all of St. Lynn's Press books may be purchased for educational, business, or sales promotional use. For information please write: Special Markets Department . St. Lynn's Press . POB 18680 . Pittsburgh, PA 15236

10 9 8 7 6 5 4 3 2 1

*With love and thanks
to my Mum, Marjorie Gibson,
who first put a trowel in my hand.*

KAREN

⌒

*To "foliage-a-holics" everywhere,
those vast numbers of gardeners who
find design inspiration first in the leaf,
then the flower.*

CHRISTINA

Table of Contents

Introduction

⁓

*A*s soon as we met at a horticultural event it was obvious we were kindred spirits. Self-confessed foliage-a-holics, the only thing we didn't have in common was that Karen couldn't limit herself to just buying foliage plants; she wanted flowers as well!

We had been traveling along parallel paths for many years as designers, speakers and writers and so it seemed a natural partnership to write this book together and share our passion for creating inspirational gardens with you. More than anything we wanted to take the mystery out of the design process and bring professional looking container gardens and landscapes within easy reach of every gardener.

Getting to "Beautiful"

Honestly – how many hours have you spent at the nursery selecting plants, only to get them home and be disappointed with the results? How *do* those designers get the look you love with such apparent ease? Rather than the magazine-perfect display you had envisioned, you seem to have flashes of brilliance one season and a hot mess in another. The results might be memorable, but not for the right reasons! So what went wrong? That's where we come in. As we explain why each of the foliage combinations on these pages is successful, you'll gain a designer's perspective to help you make great choices, take risks and create the unique garden of your dreams.

Fine Foliage goes far beyond simply offering plant names and photographs – no "shopping lists" for us! Unless you understand *why* a design works, creating new combinations can be a frustrating series of trial and error. The key to inspired design comes from careful observation of the smallest detail. Our job is to help you identify these features and expand your familiarity with the exciting world of foliage companions.

Inspiration at a Glance

This is a book you can dip into and quickly get ideas for new foliage-based combinations. The luscious photographs make it easy to identify the plants, and the key information nuggets tell you all you need to know about each plant, its care and ideal growing conditions. Consider it a resource and a reference – but most of all a springboard for your own creativity.

Fine Foliage brings an achievable level of success within easy reach, with something here for every gardener and every garden. Do you (and your plants) struggle with soaring summer temperatures? Not a problem – take a look at two of our melt-proof combinations, *Caribbean Breeze* and *Tough Love*. Prefer a sophisticated palette? You'll love the foliage blends of *Quiet Elegance* and *21st Century Vogue*. Plagued by deer? We understand your frustration and have included *Deer Be Damned* just for you! Or maybe you're a rebel at heart and like to be different: Consider us your accomplices as we show you how to break the "rules" with pizzazz in *Graceful Grasses*.

You'll discover ideas galore for containers, vignettes and entire garden borders, with the combinations often interchangeable among all three uses.

Beginners will gain confidence as they follow the simple "recipes", at the same time having the opportunity to learn why a strong framework of foliage holds the design together. Intermediate gardeners can learn how to take their skills to the next level, creating the elegant combinations that may have so far eluded them – while the experienced gardener will find fresh ideas to spark the imagination.

Designing With Foliage

The key to good design is to establish a color theme while offering diversity in texture and form – the first step in creating magic.

Color

Fine Foliage is intended to inspire you, and color is the best jumping-off point to start your new adventure. Begin by reading the color cues provided by key plants, then use them to establish color echoes with one another. Once you have your color link, vary the texture and form of the plants; that gives you a foolproof recipe for success, providing that the cultural needs of the plants are also compatible. As you gain confidence, you might introduce a new color entirely, rather than echoing one color within a combination. It could be something as simple as adding black foliage to a sweep of gold, or planting a mass of the red barberries in front of dark green conifers. Decide whether your aim is to transition into a new color scheme, to draw attention to a particular feature or to cause a scandal amongst plant critics! Use these designs as simple guideposts for you to map out your own ideas.

As you gain a deeper understanding of how to use color, your inner artist will shine – and best of all, you will avoid creating a garden that resembles Grandma's crazy quilt!

Light

Light plays an important role in how we see color. The cast of light at different times of the day, the weather and the seasons: All have an impact on color perception. Backlighting causes translucent objects to glow, creating a stunning effect. Stand underneath a golden locust tree (*Robinia pseudoacacia* 'Frisia') and bathe in an unforgettable shimmering pool of gold, or see how rich purple foliage such as that of the pansy redbud (*Cercis canadensis* 'Forest Pansy') can turn to fire when lit from behind.

Texture

In garden terms, we use the word texture to describe a surface, both visual and how it feels to the touch. The large tropical looking leaves of Rodger's flower (*Rodgersia* species) bring bold texture and drama to a scene, while maidenhair fern *(Adiantum pedatum)* and wispy leatherleaf sedge *(Carex buchananii)* offer delicate, fine textured foliage. The majority of foliage falls into the medium texture category and as such can be easily overused. Without the contrast of different textures the composition will appear unexceptional. In a small space, it is especially important that every component of a combination has to earn its place and be of value.

Leaf texture can also be described as being smooth or rough, shiny or matte, fuzzy or prickly; all of these attributes affect the depth of color. Dull, smooth leaves will not reflect light the way shiny, smooth leaves do and so will appear less intense. The aptly named mirror plant *(Coprosma repens)* sparkles like tiny jewels, and is made all the more startling when paired with the similarly colored but dull blades of Japanese blood grass *(Imperata cylindrica)*.

Children of all ages love to stroke the velvety silver leaves of the groundcover cinquefoil *(Potentilla gelida)*. It makes a wonderful rambling edging plant for the border where its soft texture can enhanced when planted adjacent to rough boulders or spiky grasses.

Form

Form refers to the overall size and shape of a plant, using terms such as mounding, columnar, vase shaped or prostrate. A garden that has "flat lines" can be dull and uninteresting, whereas adding contrast in form can be used to move the eye through a space, make a visual statement, and break up an otherwise predictable composition – rather like a loud trumpet blast in the middle of a quiet ballad! Consider a border planted with a pleasing assortment of mounding shrubs. Even with contrast in color and a mixture of fine and medium textures, this group benefits from the introduction of an upright form, especially if it sports a bold leaf, such as the impressive Empress tree *(Paulownia tomentosa),* shown here. This vertical accent asserts visual dominance as it towers over its companions and commands attention to the group.

We hope that *Fine Foliage* will help you create your own special garden magic, and have fun while you're doing it. As you pore over these luscious photographs and begin to dream of the possibilities, we know you will be inspired and excited to explore foliage in a whole new way.

Whether you're an experienced foliage fashionista or a design-challenged "crazy-quilter", our wish is that you'll soon be rushing out to your local nursery to find new treasures for your garden.

Christina & Karen

How to Use This Book

Fine Foliage is divided into two sections, Sun and Shade, giving each plant combination two full pages of identifying color photographs and text. We start every design with its glamour shot and an overview titled "Why This Works." Then we introduce you to the individual plants ("Meet the Players"), with close-up images and easy-reference details about what each one needs to thrive. Site, soil, zone, season: It's all here, along with key attributes and basic care and maintenance tips.

The foliage combinations can have as few as two plants and as many as seven. In the more complex design recipes we present the principal plants and then refer you to a "Supporting Players" page for information about the secondary plants.

As you will see, we like to name our creations. By adding a title to each design we think it will be easier for you to find your favorites again ("Now where did I see that?").

Key to the Pages

SITE

This indicates how much sun or shade the combination requires. The aim is to have plants thrive rather than just survive! Observation is vital, since an area that receives full sun in summer may be significantly more shaded in winter months, when the sun is lower.

The four variations we refer to are:

Full sun – at least 6 hours of direct sun each day

Part sun – 4-6 hours of direct sun with protection during the hottest part of the day

Part shade – areas that receive morning sun only. This often refers to the location on the eastern side of the house.

Full shade – less than 2 hours of direct sun with some filtered sun during part of the day

SOIL

Soil can vary enormously from dry sand to wet, sticky clay and everything in between; it varies across the country and within a single garden. Understanding what your soil is like and growing plants appropriate to it is the first step to successful gardening. We both constantly complain that we need a pickaxe to plant anything bigger than a daisy in our heavy clay and insist we have the WORST soil. Anyone who would beg to differ is welcome to bring a spade!

We have used the following terms to describe soil types:

Dry – Such soils drains quickly and have little organic matter

Average – Many gardeners refer to this as loam. Typically it is rich and dark, crumbles easily, and retains moisture while still allowing water to percolate through.

Well-drained – Soil does not stay saturated even after heavy rains.

Moisture retentive – Such soils are often rich in organic matter or have been mulched well with compost. Even after prolonged high temperatures these soils do not completely dry out yet neither are they waterlogged.

Wet – These soils remain wet year round e.g. stream banks.

In containers you have far more control and can adjust the level of moisture the potting soil has by changing watering frequency and/or the percentage of organic matter it contains.

ZONE

In the USA, a nationally recognized hardiness rating system (USDA) provides gardeners a way to determine which plants will survive in their geographical location based on the average annual frost-free days and minimum winter temperatures. (See the National Gardening Association's web site for helpful zone information: http://www.garden.org/zipzone/).

Zone ranges: Since individual plants within a foliage combination can have different hardiness ratings, in the zone header we give the zone range in which *all* the plants will survive (except annuals); but we also give specific hardiness information for each individual plant. Like all avid gardeners, we aren't put off simply because a label suggests that a fabulous shrub may die in our Seattle winters – we'll try it anyway! A little research at your local nurseries may help you find a perfect hardy alternative to an otherwise tender plant. Local knowledge of microclimates is invaluable.

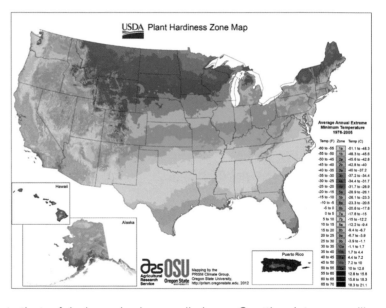

This refers to the season(s) of visual interest that the combination provides. If all plants in a group will die to the ground in winter, the season will be listed as spring-fall. If some key structural elements remain such as the interesting bark of a tree or an evergreen shrub, then it will be considered "year-round," even if one or two annuals have been included.

Definitions

We were determined from the outset that this would NOT be a book full of horticultural jargon, yet in order to create successful foliage combinations, there are certain terms it's necessary to become familiar with.

Tropical/Indoor: These terms can be confusing so we've tried to avoid their use. For simplicity, we refer to any plants that would only survive winters in zone 10 or above as annuals, even though many are suitable as houseplants or thrive in more tropical conditions.

Annual: a plant that completes its growing cycle in one season and then dies (e.g., coleus).

Perennial: a plant that may be evergreen, deciduous or herbaceous but that comes back each year (e.g., coral bells).

Herbaceous: a plant that dies to the ground in winter but re-emerges in spring (e.g., hosta).

Deciduous: a plant that loses its leaves in fall but retains its twiggy structure through winter (e.g., barberry).

Semi-evergreen: a plant that may lose a proportion of its leaves in prolonged, cold winters but will grow fresh foliage in spring (e.g., abelia).

Evergreen: a plant that keeps its leaves year-round (e.g., camellia) – although it should be noted that evergreen conifers do lose up to 1/3 of their inner foliage each year even while maintaining an evergreen appearance.

sun
COMBINATIONS

NOTE TO THE READER:

The zone header for each combination gives the range in which all the plants in the combination will survive (except annuals). Since the zone range for individual plants may extend beyond the group's, we note each plant's hardiness range as well.

LUSCIOUS LAYERS

WHY THIS WORKS

This combination is all about layering, with each tier of foliage resting lightly on its partner. As the branches and blades mingle, the subtle details are accentuated and can be better appreciated: the fascinating zigzag pattern on the large bellwort stems, the perfect heart-shaped leaves from the tree, and the arching blades of grass, each brushed lightly with a stroke of creamy-yellow. Who is the greater artist...Nature or the landscape designer?

MEET THE PLAYERS

'FOREST PANSY' REDBUD
(*Cercis canadensis* 'Forest Pansy')

A year-round performer, this deciduous tree is a "must have" if you can find a spot sheltered from strong winds. Growing 15-25' tall and wide, it adds clusters of pink flowers to the spring garden followed by striking purple heart-shaped leaves. Fall sees the canopy ignite into fiery shades of red and gold, and even the stark winter silhouette offers interest. Zones 6-9

LARGE BELLWORT
(*Uvularia grandiflora*)

Long, oval leaves appear to have been sewn together by a child using large zigzag stiches. This moisture loving herbaceous perennial grows 2-3' tall in light shade – if the deer don't find it first! Yellow bell-shaped flowers hang from the stems in May. Zones 4-9

VARIEGATED PURPLE MOOR GRASS
(*Molinia caerulea* subsp. *caerulea* 'Variegata')

This compact perennial forms dense clumps of slender green leaves marked with creamy-yellow stripes. In summer, arching flower stalks rise to 3' tall, each inflorescence holding well into the fall as it fades to tan. A lush and beautiful grass, it grows best in full sun or partial shade and needs rich, moist soil. Cut the grass to the ground in fall once it yellows. Zones 5-9

LETHAL BEAUTY

WHY THIS WORKS

Stout work gloves may be needed to plant this combination, but the effect is well worth a few scratches! Redleaf rose has delicate, single pink flowers reminiscent of an old-fashioned dog rose, but it is the glaucus foliage accented by rosy hued stems, midribs and thorns that makes this a perfect color partner for the pink-splashed barberry behind.

MEET THE PLAYERS

REDLEAF ROSE
(Rosa glauca)

Vivid pink flowers are followed by attractive hips. But what really gives this plant its place in the mixed border is its 6' fountain of blue-green foliage. If the rose gets too big, simply cut it back; new, strong canes will quickly emerge – no fancy pruning required. This rose will self-seed, but if not wanted, they are easy to remove. Planting this in full sun or light shade and giving it some elbow room will help to keep the foliage disease-free. Zones 2-8

'ROSE GLOW' BARBERRY
(Berberis thunbergii 'Rose Glow')

This tough, thorny shrub mirrors the arching form and size of the redleaf rose, while offering a painterly effect with its marbled leaves in shades of pink, white and purple. In autumn, the entire shrub turns scarlet before the leaves drop. No pruning is necessary. A great easy-care addition to the garden. Zones 4-8

A THREE-LEAF TRIFECTA

WHY THIS WORKS

Three foliage types blend the same leaf size and texture to create a feast for the eyes. The tightly planted combination of perennial and shrubs is worth noting for three reasons: dramatic differences in foliage color, harmonious growth habits, and the elegant way they take turns with seasonal color changes throughout the year. When the cool fall season temperatures arrive, the barberry takes the lead and all three plants transform into a colorful but tidy frenzy.

MEET THE PLAYERS

'TRICOLOR' SAGE
(Salvia officinalis 'Tricolor')

Cooks and garden designers alike appreciate this semi-evergreen perennial for its unique flavor, aroma, and colorful array of leaves. The gray-green, white-margined leaves, suffused with pink or purple, are at their dramatic best in fall and winter. In early summer, lavender flower spikes emerge to the delight of butterflies. It forms a 1.5' tall bush with woody stems. Trim back to newly emerging growth or strong stems in spring to encourage bushiness. Zones 6-9

'GULF STREAM' HEAVENLY BAMBOO
(Nandina domestica 'Gulf Stream')

This outstanding evergreen shrub displays distinctive foliage in all seasons. New growth is scarlet, maturing to blue-green in summer. Its hallmark is the intense red color that comes after a cold snap. Moderately fast growing, its dense, mounded form reaches to 3.5' tall and 3' wide, making 'Gulf Stream' ideal for use around foundations or in mixed borders. The small white flower stalks are a bonus. Zones 6-11

'CRIMSON PYGMY' BARBERRY
(Berberis thunbergii var. *atropurpurea* 'Crimson Pygmy')

This barberry is a versatile, low profile red-leafed shrub adaptable to many garden needs. With noteworthy fall color and tiny red berries up and down the length of its dark red stems in winter, it carries its weight in the garden for year-round design. Zones 4-8

BALANCING ACT

WHY THIS WORKS

Certainly the metallic finish of this container helps to dictate the harmonious color story of this design. It is the texture of this foliage that balances the bold with the detailed. The dark stems of the hebe echo the rich, jewel-like colors of the hen and chicks, while the bright golden-yellow Cape fuchsia makes a bold statement to contrast with the strappiness of New Zealand flax. Pulling it all together is the tri-color balancing act of the spurge. (The flax is a "Supporting Player," shown on page 126.)

MEET THE PLAYERS

'SUNSHINE' CAPE FUCHSIA
(Phygelius x rectus 'Sunshine')

This form of Cape fuchsia is a stunner in pale gold. It blooms for months, from summer to fall, with long, pink, tubular flowers that are a hummingbird and butterfly favorite. A fast grower, it will reach 36-48" tall and wide in partial shade to full sun.
Zones 7-10

'CHAMPION' HEBE
(Hebe 'Champion')

In the varied forms of hebe, 'Champion' is a favorite performer for many gardeners. The small cup-shaped leaves, dark stems and violet-lavender summer blooms work well in many design styles. At just 12-18" tall and 18-24" wide, it is also well suited to alpine gardens. Zones 7-11

'ASCOT RAINBOW' SPURGE
(Euphorbia x martinii 'Ascot Rainbow')

This is a perfect plant whenever you need it, with green, fluffy spring blooms and foliage in golds, chartreuse, pinks and bronze. Grows 18-24" tall and wide in part to full sun. Hardy in well-drained soil.
Zones 7-10
CAUTION: Skin irritant; wear gloves when handling this plant.

HEN AND CHICKS
(Sempervivum tectorum)

A favorite plant for its ease and quirkiness, this plant is available in many colors and sizes for rock gardens, xeriscapes or containers. Sempervivum are prolific, colonizing freely. It blooms with rosettes that can be pink or yellow, and in full sun this plant will be up to 6" tall and 12" wide. Zones 4-8

DEER BE DAMNED!

WHY THIS WORKS

Attention to detail and complete deer resistance make this design a winner for both containers and gardens. The black, shiny container provides the inspiration: The color is repeated by the elderberry foliage, silver wormwood emphasizes the glossy finish, green and white variegated foliage plants lighten the mood, and the field scabious leaves make a dramatic focal point. The soft pink coral bells draw attention to the barberry stems for a punch of color. (Elderberry is shown on page 126.)

MEET THE PLAYERS

'LIME GLOW' BARBERRY
(Berberis thunbergii 'Lime Glow')

This new barberry offers a subtle blend of mid-green, chartreuse and white-splashed foliage on a 5' vase-shaped shrub. In fall, the addition of red berries creates drama. Resistant to sunburn. Zones 4-7

'PINOT GRIS' CORAL BELLS
(Heuchera villosa 'Pinot Gris')

One of the compact coral bells, at 12" wide, this new variety thrives in sun or part shade. The ever-green pale ginger leaves are overlaid with silver, giving it a gentle metallic sheen. These age to smoky-rose with a purple reverse. Zones 4-9

'THUNDER AND LIGHTNING' FIELD SCABIOUS
(Knautia macedonica 'Thunder and Lightning')

Dramatic green and white variegated foliage provides the backdrop for magenta "pincushion" flowers in summer. Compact and drought tolerant, this herbaceous perennial is a winner. 15" tall and 18" wide. Zones 4-7

'SILVER MOUND' WORMWOOD
(Artemisia schmidtiana 'Nana')

Who can resist touching this soft, feathery silver cushion? Great for hot, dry sites, this perennial can be sheared mid-summer if it gets straggly and will quickly rebound. Divide every 2-3 years in spring. 12" tall and 18" wide. Zones 4-8

A CHANGE OF PACE

WHY THIS WORKS

Succulent-driven design has become increasingly popular over the past few years, so it is refreshing to see them being combined with something different. The gentle movement of the tall, slender bamboo canes brings welcome relief to the solid mass of fleshier foliage. The arching leaves of Lily of the Nile also help to soften the scene, while introducing a new shape.

MEET THE PLAYERS

LILY OF THE NILE
(Agapanthus cultivar)

Usually grown for its late summer starry blue flowers, the green strap-like foliage of this unknown cultivar is also very attractive. Evergreen and herbaceous cultivars are available, all of which are typically hardy in zones 8-11.

BLACK ROSE
(Aeonium arboreum var. *atropurpureum* 'Zwartkop')

Rosettes of glossy, black succulent foliage stand tall on sturdy 18" stems. Enjoy them in the garden for the summer, but overwinter indoors. Needs full sun and well drained soil. Annual

'GARNET' AEONIUM
(Aeonium 'Garnet')

Green, fleshy rosettes heavily tipped in dark red grow to form a dense carpet 1-3' tall. Best color in full sun and needs well drained soil. Annual

GOLDEN BAMBOO
(Phyllostachys aurea cultivar)

Several cultivars of golden bamboo are available which share a similar running habit, so be sure to use a rhizome barrier to keep this beauty in check! All typically grow 25-30' tall and are evergreen, with most being hardy in zones 7-10.

HARMONY

WHY THIS WORKS

Nature leads the design in this Asian inspired garden. Restraint in the color palette is balanced with an emphasis on weaving together a tapestry of textures. Majestic trees form the backdrop, layered in front with yellow bamboo and evergreen shrubs, all skirted with a waterfall of soft yellow Japanese forest grass and the mounding form of a Japanese maple – a peaceful harmony of Nature and man-made beauty.

MEET THE PLAYERS

WESTERN RED CEDAR
(Thuja plicata)

This fast growing conifer is easily recognized by its drooping branches from which feathery foliage drapes. The scale-like foliage is highly fragrant when crushed and the bark is soft and shaggy. To 190' tall and 40' wide. Zones 5-8

'CRIMSON QUEEN' JAPANESE MAPLE
(Acer palmatum var. dissectum 'Crimson Queen')

An elegant, mounding tree with finely dissected foliage in shades of burnished bronze and burgundy. Brilliant red fall color. Grows to 10' tall x 13' wide. Zones 5-8

'GREEN GROOVE' BAMBOO
(Phyllostachys aureosulcata 'Spectabilis')

A sturdy rhizome barrier is needed to keep this bamboo in check. It quickly forms a dense thicket of 2" yellow canes, each striped with green, which reach 30' high. It typically has a zigzag habit. In more sun the new growth is bright red. Zones 6-10

JAPANESE FOREST GRASS
(Hakonechloa macra 'Aureola')

One of the most popular low growing grasses, the cascading soft yellow foliage is perfect for the front of the border or container. An herbaceous perennial to 3' x 3'. Zones 5-9

BERRY-LICIOUS

WHY THIS WORKS

A mouthwatering confection for a partially sunny spot. Berry-hued foliage accented with a little frill of silver: perhaps this should be planted in an oversized sundae dish? Simple color echoes, together with the fresh texture introduced by the hebe, make this a delicious combination for containers or edging a border.

MEET THE PLAYERS

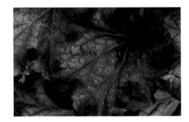

'BERRY SMOOTHIE' CORAL BELLS
(Heuchera 'Berry Smoothie')

A year round winner, this ever-green perennial glows with bright raspberry shades in spring, deep-ening to vibrant marionberry as the season progresses. This adapt-able cultivar will take full sun to full shade, providing the soil does not dry out, and is known for its heat and humidity tolerance. 18" tall and wide. Zones 4-9

'CROWN JEWEL' CORAL BELLS
(Heuchera 'Crown Jewel')

The perfect size to tuck into a corner, this dwarf coral bells may only be 12" tall but what it lacks in size it makes up for in interest. The silvery-hued foliage is ruffled like a petticoat, revealing the purple underneath. It prefers full or partial shade, so plant it where it will be protected from the sun by other plants. Zones 4-9

'QUICKSILVER' HEBE
(Hebe pimeleoides 'Quicksilver')

The open, airy habit of this low growing evergreen shrub makes an exciting contrast to the dense mounding forms of its companions. Tiny blue-gray leaves are held stiffly along black wiry stems and are adorned with small lilac-colored flowers in early summer. Full to partial sun. Zones 7-11

A MAGICAL JOURNEY

WHY THIS WORKS

This garden measures only 21' x 12', yet the meandering path takes you on a magical journey past billowing shrubs in shades of purple and gold. A simple stacked stone sculpture beckons to a turn in the path, and drama is added by the bold visual exclamation point of the Empress tree. Each artful layer of texture invites exploration. (Three of the seven plants are "Supporting Players," shown on page 126.)

MEET THE PLAYERS

'BENI OTAKE' JAPANESE MAPLE
(Acer palmatum 'Beni otake')

The strap-like bronze foliage of this elegant maple frames the stone sculpture and adds a translucent canopy to this outdoor room, creating a sense of intimacy. This sun tolerant maple turns crimson in fall and grows to 10' tall and wide. Zones 6-9

'OGON' OR 'MELLOW YELLOW' SPIREA
(Spiraea thunbergii 'Ogon')

Forming a loose mound of golden, feathery foliage 5' wide and tall, this easy care deciduous shrub thrives in full sun or light shade. Fall color is orange. It can be trimmed to keep smaller if preferred. Zones 4-8

'BOWLES' GOLDEN SEDGE
(Carex elata 'Aurea')

Although this grass is said to be evergreen, it benefits from being cut back in spring. The bright yellow foliage forms 2' fountains. It thrives in the moist soil and partial shade beneath the smoke bush. Zones 5-9

'VELVET CLOAK' SMOKE BUSH
(Cotinus coggygria 'Velvet Cloak')

This deciduous shrub has stunning deep purple foliage that turns orange-red in autumn. Flowers are followed by long lasting plume-like seed heads, creating the namesake smoke. 10-15' tall and wide if not pruned. Zones 4-8

| SITE: Full sun | SEASON: Year-round | SOIL: Average, moisture retentive | ZONE: 9-11 |

CARIBBEAN BREEZE

WHY THIS WORKS

Sit back with your favorite fruity cocktail and imagine you're in the Tropics with this exotic trio on your patio. Since each plant has palm-like foliage, it's up to diversity of color to make this combination really pop. Add a bold citrus backdrop and you'll be reaching for the sunglasses!

MEET THE PLAYERS

MAJESTY PALM
(Ravenea rivularis)

In tropical climates this fast growing palm can reach over 40' tall and 6-8' wide, but in temperate zones it can be enjoyed as a more modestly sized indoor plant, with a summer vacation to the patio. Provide consistently moist soil in full sun or partial shade. Zones 9-11

BAUER'S DRACAENA PALM
(Cordyline 'Baueri')

This slender tree is a great palm alternative for smaller spaces, at 8-10' tall and 5' wide. A cluster of burgundy, sword-shaped blades seems to explode from the trunk like a bold feather duster, while in summer fragrant white flowers add to the display. Remove older leaves as needed. Grow in full sun or partial shade and do not allow the soil to dry out. Zones 9-11

'GARLAND GOLD'
ADAM'S NEEDLE
(Yucca filamentosa 'Garland Gold')

Each broad, green, leathery blade is accented with brilliant gold bands. When mature, these evergreen rosettes produce a tall spike loaded with large, fragrant, white flowers in late summer. This evergreen shrub is slow growing to 3' x 3', is deer resistant and will tolerate dry soils. Wear stout gloves to divide clumps every 5-6 years. Zones 5-11

BLUES ON FIRE!

WHY THIS WORKS

This photo illustrates how important a background can be in tying a foliage palette together. The designer repeated the fiery backdrop color in front, using the bold coral bells to catch the eye. The subtle and layered cool blues are a sophisticated and textural foliage interplay too, especially with the use of the fantastic blueberry! (See page 126 of "Supporting Players" for blue switch grass, not shown here.)

MEET THE PLAYERS

'BABY BLUE' FALSE CYPRESS
(Chamaecyparis pisifera 'Baby Blue')

The ultra-soft blue foliage with silvery overtones on this false cypress is a winning combination, enhanced by a lavender blush in winter. It is also a fabulous option for a drought tolerant garden. 6' tall and 4' wide.
Zones 4-8

'GLACIER BLUE' SPURGE
(Euphorbia characias 'Glacier Blue')

Bringing drama to the garden, this deer resistant perennial showcases creamy-white edged foliage which acts as a foil for the clusters of spring flowers that bloom white with a green eye. This drought tolerant plant grows to 30" tall and wide. Zones 7-11
CAUTION: Skin irritant

'REGINA' CORAL BELLS
(Heuchera 'Regina')

Coral bells are an indispensable addition to any garden. This one features leaves that are a rich burgundy with a shimmery silver overlay and purple undersides, plus airy, pale pink flowers in summer. 1-2' tall and wide.
Zones 4-9

'BOUNTIFUL BLUE' BLUEBERRY
(Vaccinium corymbosum 'Bountiful Blue')

This new blueberry is a prolific producer of sweet berries and does not require a partner plant for production, but will make more berries if there is. Consistent water, annual fertilizing with an acidic fertilizer and spring pruning make this 3-4' tall and wide beauty a landscape must. Zones 6-10

DOUBLE DUTY DESIGN

WHY THIS WORKS

Foliage combinations like this one truly earn their place in the landscape or container by performing over and above the call of duty from spring through fall. As fall arrives, Virginia sweetspire really starts to put on a show as the foliage glows in shades of crimson and scarlet, creating a striking partnership with the blushing weigela. The steel-blue tones of the lyme grass add a cooling note to this otherwise fiery display.

MEET THE PLAYERS

'LITTLE HENRY' DWARF VIRGINIA SWEETSPIRE
(Itea virginica 'Little Henry')

This dwarf shrub grows 2-3' tall and wide and prefers consistently moist soils. Noted for its heavy spring bloom and fiery fall color, sweetspire is an easy care, high performance shrub. Zones 5-9

'BLUE DUNE' LYME GRASS
(Elymus arenarius 'Blue Dune')

The cool blue color of this beachy, casual grass is striking in the garden. As a fast-growing evergreen plant to 2' tall and wide, it's a great choice for weed control in an area where drought tolerant plants are needed. Hardy in zones 4-9

'MY MONET' WEIGELA
(Weigela florida 'My Monet')

Pale-pink spring flowers, together with green, white and pink variegated foliage from spring to fall, make this dwarf, deciduous shrub a winner. It grows only 12-18" tall and wide,so you should never really have to prune it! Weigela also get big points for its deer resistant status as well. Zones 4-7

| SITE: Full sun | SEASON: Spring-Fall | SOIL: Average, well-drained | ZONE: 5-7 |

LEAF PATTERN PARADIGM

WHY THIS WORKS

This combination beautifully illustrates the design paradigm of threes. The trio here shows small, medium and large foliage; you could also describe it as fine, medium and course texture. Their color harmony is from three basic colors: green, burgundy and off-white. As this combination matures, it will continue the pattern, with individual growth habits being low, mid and taller heights. This design will only be enhanced by the early and late season blooms and tremendous fall color.

MEET THE PLAYERS

'CRIMSON PYGMY' BARBERRY
(Berberis thunbergii var. atropurpurea 'Crimson Pygmy')

This dwarf barberry at 3' tall x 3' wide is a hardy and a drought tolerant option for many parts of the country. Its foliage, berries and tremendous fall color are invaluable in the landscape.
Zones 4-9

'AUTUMN CHARM' STONECROP, SEDUM
(Sedum hylotelephium)

A truly charming upright sedum. The foliage colors alone would be enough, even if it never bloomed! The drought and heat tolerance factors are big benefits in a low maintenance landscape. This sedum is one that deer won't bother but butterflies will adore.
Zones 3-9

'PINK BEAUTY' CINQUEFOIL
(Potentilla fruticosa 'Pink Beauty')

A slow growing, deciduous shrub, it matures at about 3' high and wide, and blooms prolifically in spring. It may look delicate, but once established will be cold and drought hardy. Bonus points for deer resistance – and fall color that will knock your socks off.
Zones 3-7

SITE: Full sun	SEASON: Spring-Fall	SOIL: Average, well-drained	ZONE: 7-8

IN THE LIMELIGHT

WHY THIS WORKS

Drawing your eye straight into the center of this combination is the core of the design: the black rose. With its broad leaves and radial growth habit, it is the perfect contrast to the finer textures surrounding it. While a riot of different foliage in such a small space might seem to be a distraction, the contemporary color scheme, bold shapes and strong design pull it together. (This design's three "Supporting Players" are shown on page 127.)

MEET THE PLAYERS

BLACK ROSE
(Aeonium arboreum var. *atropurpureum* 'Zwartkop')*

An eye catching succulent, its glossy black foliage grows as rosettes on 18" stems. It needs well drained soil and prefers full sun. Enjoy indoors during colder months.
Annual

ASPARAGUS FERN
(Asparagus sprengeri)

This fluffy cousin of the edible asparagus is an annual in colder areas and a foundation plant in warmer climates. At 2' tall by 3-4' wide and preferring moderate water, this plant is flexible for both container and garden designs. Large thorns protect its beautiful but highly toxic berries.
Zones 9-11

'KEY LIME PIE' CORAL BELLS
(Heuchera 'Key Lime Pie')*

This attractive chartreuse foliage brightens any shady garden or container. Evergreen or semi-evergreen depending on your climate, this coral bells will grow 16" tall and 12"wide, producing spikes of pink flowers in summer.
Zones 4-9

'TOFFEE TWIST' HAIR SEDGE
(Carex flagellifera 'Toffee Twist')*

The slender foliage of this evergreen grass is great for fitting into tight spaces in containers or as showy texture in the garden. The rich brown color plays well with both warm and cool shades. 2' tall and wide.
Zones 7-10

A THUG, A BULLY AND A GENTLE GIANT

WHY THIS WORKS

This pond is a natural wonder, to be sure, and designing at the water's edge is a challenge. Our plant palette is full of creative genius with the use of true "colonizer" plants, to put it politely. Each of these is happy to withstand the wet and muck. The grass and umbrella plant are a natural born pair of rival gang members that want each other's turf, while the cypress tree stands tall and acts as referee over the action.

MEET THE PLAYERS

POND CYPRESS
(Taxodium ascendens)

One of the few deciduous conifers, the pond cypress has bright green feathery foliage that turns to shades of rust in fall. It will grow to 80' tall and 15' wide and thrives in boggy areas. Zones 5-9

VARIEGATED RIBBON GRASS, GARDENERS GARTERS
(Phalaris arundinacea 'Picta')

A grass with the constitution and bad manners of bamboo! The pretty variegation and soft airy flowers belie its thuggish person-ality. It will spread aggressively, especially in wet soil. Cut to the ground in winter.
Zones 3-9

UMBRELLA PLANT
(Darmera peltata)

This is another herbaceous peren-nial that spreads rapidly. Naked flower stalks appear in spring with clusters of starry pale pink flowers, followed by large, dinner-plate-sized leaves. Although typically grown in partial shade, this healthy specimen is thriving in full sun, possibly because it is planted in very wet soil. 4' tall. Zones 5-7

DESIGN, DIVIDE, REPEAT

WHY THIS WORKS

This beguiling trio of plants may look deceptively simple from a design standpoint, but it's in fact a quite brilliantly executed example of the use of subtle color hues melded with textural interest and dollar value. By keeping this combination to only these three plants, the repetition makes THE statement. Plus, you can divide two of these plants every couple of years – a fantastic investment.

MEET THE PLAYERS

'SILVER KING' EUONYMUS
(Euonymus japonica 'Silver King')

The foliage coloration on this particular cultivar of euonymus is a creamy, smooth, rich tone that plays well off similarly colored plants; not too bold, not too soft. As an easy going hedge plant it's simple to prune, and in a container easy to keep to desired size. Evergreen and loving full sun, this plant will grow to 6' tall and 3' wide. Zones 6-9

'PLUM PUDDING' CORAL BELLS
(Heuchera 'Plum Pudding')

Rich and velvety, just like plum pudding, it's the perfect name for this evergreen perennial. Bold veining and a slight silvery tinge to the leaves make this interesting to grow year round. At 1-3' tall and wide, the mounding habit is a valuable contribution to the front of the border or a container. Zones 4-9

DWARF VARIEGATED PAMPAS GRASS
(Cortaderia selloana 'Splendid Star')

The creamy-yellow variegation is subtle yet rich in full sun, with apricot tones in fall. It's an ideal choice for smaller landscapes at only 3-5' tall, compared to its full-sized cousin. Silvery-white plumes appear in late summer for dramatic winter interest. Drought-tolerant but prefers fertile, well drained soil. Wear stout gloves to cut back old flowering stems in spring. Evergreen in zones 7-9

GRACEFUL GRASSES

WHY THIS WORKS

When designing plant combinations we usually vary the leaf shape for interest. Yet by planting large drifts of each grass, while adding contrast in both color and form, this sweeping prairie-style border makes a powerful statement – even without the addition of the rosy-colored sedum, seen in the foreground. All plants are easy care and deer resistant. (See "Supporting Players," page 126, for blue fescue.)

MEET THE PLAYERS

JAPANESE BLOOD GRASS
(Imperata cylindrica)

An herbaceous grass that is grown for its striking red-tipped, vertical blades. It reaches 2' tall but will spread aggressively and is considered invasive in some areas. Zones 4-9

'BLAZE OF FULDA' SEDUM
(Sedum spurium 'Blaze of Fulda')

This semi-evergreen succulent is a favorite both as a groundcover and in containers. Deep red foliage acts as a foil for the bright pink summer flowers. 4" tall with a spreading habit. Zones 4-9

MEXICAN FEATHER GRASS
(Stipa tenuissima)

This evergreen grass brings movement to the scene, its loose, wispy fountains swaying gently in even the slightest breeze. It is considered invasive in some areas due to self-seeding. 2' tall and wide. Zones 6-10

'BOWLES' GOLDEN SEDGE
(Carex elata 'Aurea')

Vivid golden foliage glows in full sun or partial shade. It is semi-evergreen and benefits from trimming in spring to allow the fresh growth to shine. Best in average-wet soil. 1' tall and wide. Zones 5-9

FATAL ATTRACTION

WHY THIS WORKS

Just like fearless moths, we are naturally drawn to bright lights, and this combination is no exception. The soft feathery mound of the conifer beckons like a golden teddy bear, but beware its highly attractive partner. Try stroking those leathery blades and you'll get a sharp surprise. These two plants may share a similar color yet display a strong contrast in form and texture. Look but don't touch!

MEET THE PLAYERS

ADAM'S NEEDLE
(Yucca filamentosa 'Color Guard')

A dramatic evergreen shrub that grows slowly to 3' x 3'. Each broad spiny blade is streaked with gold, with each rosette producing a tall spike of fragrant white flowers in summer. Zones 5-11
CAUTION: Wear gloves to divide every 5-6 years.

THREADLEAF FALSECYPRESS 'GOLDEN MOPS'
(Chamaecyparis pisifera 'Filifera Aurea')

The thread-like golden foliage of this evergreen conifer creates a large mound providing four season interest. It may reach 10' or more tall and wide but can be pruned to keep smaller. Full sun or afternoon shade. Hardiness ratings vary, but generally accepted for zones 5-9.

ALL THAT GLITTERS

WHY THIS WORKS

Glittering in the late afternoon sun, silver and gold foliage becomes a natural focal point. The ruby-colored grass adds variety to the treasure chest by introducing a fresh texture and shape, while adding another jewel to the collection.

MEET THE PLAYERS

JAPANESE SNOWBELL
(Styrax japonica)

A delightful small tree best known for its delicate bell-shaped white flowers in June, which perfume the air before falling like confetti. Even without flowers, this is an attractive tree, having a tidy pyramidal shape and mid-green leaves that turn to gold in fall. 15-25' tall and wide. Zones 5-8

RUSSIAN OLIVE
(Elaeagnus angustifolia 'Quick Silver')

With its elliptical silvery-gray leaves, this fast growing shrub is sure to be noticed. When grown in constantly moist soil this will quickly reach 30-40' tall and 12-15' wide. Yellow, fragrant flowers are followed in fall by small fruit. Zones 2-9

CAUTION: sharp spines

JAPANESE BLOOD GRASS
(Imperata cylindrica)

This herbaceous grass has erect olive-green blades tipped in burgundy, which intensifies as the season progresses. This will spread rapidly, especially in moist soil and is considered invasive in some areas. To 2' tall and hardy in zones 4-9.

GOLDBLOTCH GLADIOLI
(Gladiolus papilio)

A rare gem for the collector, this gladioli is like no other! The 2' mound of herbaceous grassy foliage throws up arching stems in late summer, each topped with a row of 1-2" dusky lilac blooms. Happy in moisture retentive soil – sometimes too happy! Hardy in zones 8-11.

CURTAIN CALL

WHY THIS WORKS

Towering grasses are the curtains against which the actors perform. The star of this production is clearly the ornamental rhubarb with its steroidal presence. Yet, such monster-sized plants need companions that can hold their own in some way – and a froth of chartreuse pierced by burgundy blades balances the scene with flair.

MEET THE PLAYERS

MALEPARTUS MAIDEN GRASS
(Miscanthus sinensis 'Malepartus')

At 4-8' tall and 2-4' wide, this fast growing grass will hold its own against the ornamental rhubarb. Arching green blades each have a silvery-white midrib, while summer flowers open pink but gradually fade to silver. In fall, the foliage takes on orange, red and bronze hues. Zones 5-9

ORNAMENTAL RHUBARB
(Rheum palmatum 'Atrosanguineum')

This perennial asks only for water and serious elbow room. In spring, cherry red buds unfurl to release the oversized coarse leaves – green on the upper side and striking burgundy below. Growing rapidly to 8' tall and wide, it creates quite the talking point! Zones 3-8

PINEAPPLE LILY
(Eucomis comosa 'Sparkling Burgundy')

Smooth, burgundy, sword-like foliage points dramatically skyward. In summer, thick stalks are topped by flowers that resemble pineapples. This herbaceous perennial grows 1-2' tall and wide and is hardy in zones 8-10; possibly colder in dry conditions.

LADY'S MANTLE
(Alchemilla mollis)

Velvety leaves hold water droplets so beautifully you could almost wish for rain! Clusters of tiny chartreuse flowers are held above the foliage in summer, creating a pretty, frothy effect. It is best to remove these seed heads to prevent prolific self-seeding. This perennial grows 1' tall and wide. Zones 4-8

EASY ON THE EYES

WHY THIS WORKS

Soft, upward facing spikes unite these two shrubs in gentle harmony. The silvery-gray foliage of the lavender cotton draws attention to the pale stripes on the underside of each pine needle. This pairing is understated yet balanced; the gentle color palette could be used to link more extrovert plants.

MEET THE PLAYERS

'BLUE SHAG' PINE
(Pinus strobus 'Blue Shag')

As soft as a teddy bear, this mounding conifer grows slowly into a 3-4' dome. Gorgeous in a large bowl-shaped container or in the landscape. Gently shake out inner needles in spring, as they turn brown. Zones 3-8

LAVENDER COTTON
(Santolina chamaecyparissus)

This 2' tall evergreen shrub is tough: drought tolerant, deer resistant and will thrive in the poorest of soils. In summer, bright yellow button-like flowers brighten the aromatic gray foliage. Cut back hard if it begins to look straggly. Zones 6-9

QUIET ELEGANCE

WHY THIS WORKS

Simplicity is the key to this enchanting design. Gorgeous heart-shaped leaves from the 'Forest Pansy' redbud set the scene with shades of warm purple fading to soft green. The coral bells echo these shades and introduce cool silver to the color story, while spiky, silvery-blue mounds of blue fescue grass add a new leaf shape. To complete the vignette, a skirt of succulent foliage brings all these shades together. ('October Daphne' stonecrop is a "Supporting Player," shown on page 126.)

MEET THE PLAYERS

'FOREST PANSY' REDBUD
(Cercis canadensis 'Forest Pansy')

This stunning deciduous tree grows to 15-25' tall and wide. It is truly a four season star with clusters of pink spring flowers appearing before the heart-shaped leaves. The striking purple foliage turns to fiery shades of gold and ruby in fall. Though deciduous, its attractive branching silhouette still adds interest to the winter garden. Exposed, windy locations are best avoided as the branches tend to be brittle. Zones 6-9

BLUE FESCUE GRASS
(Festuca glauca)

Evergreen foliage, drought tolerance and disease resistance make this an easy-care grass. Growing to 12" tall and wide, these tidy hummocks throw up delicate, tawny flower spikes in summer. If allowed to set seed, these will produce new plants nearby, but are easily removed if preferred. Gently raking your fingers through the tufts in spring helps to remove congested older blades, leaving behind the fresher foliage and encouraging new growth. Zones 3-9

'DOLCE BLACKCURRANT' CORAL BELLS
(Heuchera 'Dolce Blackcurrant')

These coral bells thrive in woodland gardens, so are right at home nestled under the redbud tree. Evergreen leaves in luscious shades of silver and burgundy are further enhanced by raspberry tones on the undersides, glimpsed occasionally at their ruffled edges. Care is minimal – snip off older, brown leaves as necessary. In spring, spires of delicate white flowers decorate the plants. 2' tall and 1' wide. Zones 4-9

FOLIAGE FIESTA!

WHY THIS WORKS

Parties are all about mingling, making new friends and having fun, and these three beauties do that with style! Grouping individually potted plants allows for flexibility and is a great way to experiment. Here, the bright mosaic of the coleus vies for attention with the exotic looking canna, while New Zealand flax adds a change of shape with its strong upright blades. These three variegated plants share the same fiery colors, yet vary in texture and form. It's fiesta time!

MEET THE PLAYERS

CANNA 'TROPICANNA'
(Canna x generalis 'Tropicanna')

One of the most popular cannas, this beauty easily reaches 5' or more in height when its blowsy orange flowers push skyward. The colorful foliage is what makes it a real winner, however, as the stripes of red, orange and gold glow like hot embers when backlit by the sun. Provide regular summer water but avoid winter wet. Zones 7-11

'FINGER PAINT' COLEUS
(Solenostemon scutellarioides 'Finger paint')

A fun, sun loving, heat tolerant coleus with an upright habit. The leaves do indeed look like a child's artwork with finger-sized splotches of red and yellow. 2' tall and wide. Annual

'GOLDEN RAY' NEW ZEALAND FLAX
(Phormium tenax 'Golden Ray')

This evergreen shrub grows 4-5' tall and wide. The broad blades have a central olive-green band surrounded by creamy yellow and edged with orange. Avoid winter wet and it will be hardy in zones 7-11.

RICH AND REGAL

WHY THIS WORKS

Rich colors and exciting textures make this a sublime combination. Each of the elements – from the whisper-soft gossamer sedge to the layers of taffeta from the coral bells, the ruffled layers of hydrangea foliage to the silky cypress that just begs you to run your fingers through its tight curls – is woven together to create a textile fit for royalty.

MEET THE PLAYERS

'GOLDRUSH' HYDRANGEA

(Hydrangea macrophylla goldrush)

'Goldrush' produces an abundance of lace-cap pink flowers that make a bright contrast with the lemon-yellow variegated foliage. This deciduous shrub has a compact bushy habit at 4-5' tall and wide and is a favorite of butterflies and humming-birds. Zones 6-9

'CURLY TOP' DWARF SAWARA CYPRESS

(Chamaecyparis pisifera 'Curly Top')

The contorted or curly blue foliage on this compact conifer is both fun and dramatic. Growing 3-6' tall and wide in full to partial sun, this cypress is an easy plant for adding bold color in a small space. Zones 4-8

ORANGE HAIR SEDGE

(Carex testacea)

This is a wonderful evergreen grass whose wispy, olive-green blades are tipped with bronze, a color that intensifies as fall approaches. At 16" tall and 12" wide, it is perfect for containers or the landscape and thrives in sun or partial shade. Zones 7-10

'SOUTHERN COMFORT' CORAL BELLS

(Heuchera villosa 'Southern Comfort')

Named for its deep Southern roots, this heat and humidity tolerant evergreen has a radiance of cinnamon-peach, with new growth a glowing amber in spring. Grows 14" tall and 24" wide. Zones 4-9

MASTERPIECE

WHY THIS WORKS

This is one of those picture-perfect scenes that you could never grow tired of. A rainbow of Nature's colors is reflected in the water, an artist's delight of echoing beauty. Bringing the distant autumnal shades into focus is the tiered wedding cake tree with its green and white variegated foliage. By planting this specimen tree in the foreground a greater sense of depth is achieved. Truly a work of art.

MEET THE PLAYERS

WEDDING CAKE TREE
(Cornus controversa 'Variegata')

Resembling tiers of a wedding cake, this graceful tree displays branches in a distinctive layered manner. Boldly variegated green and white leaves turn purple in fall, while clusters of white flowers in summer are a bonus. Even in winter, its silhouette is striking. Prefers full sun and moisture retentive soil. 20' tall x 20' wide. Zones 4-8

CORAL BARK MAPLE
(Acer palmatum 'Sango-kaku')

One of the most popular Japanese maples, this displays bright green leaves delicately edged with red, which turn golden in fall. Pair that with brilliant coral-colored bark and you have a year round star. 20' tall and wide in full sun or part shade. Zones 5-8

PURPLE WAVES

WHY THIS WORKS

Placing the soft, feathery grass adjacent to spiky, purple barberry provides contrast in texture and form, yet offers a subtle repetition of color. A carpet of silvery wormwood lends a romantic picture frame to the scheme, and since all three plants are extremely drought tolerant and deer resistant, they make excellent cultural companions as well as design partners.

MEET THE PLAYERS

PURPLE FOUNTAIN GRASS
(Pennisetum setaceum 'Rubrum')

The narrow, curving foliage has a rich burgundy cast, while the pink, purple and tan foxtail-like flowers rise above this soft mound on slender stems to sway gently in the breeze. 3-4' tall. Zones 8-11

'ROSE GLOW' BARBERRY
(Berberis thunbergii 'Rose Glow')

This thorny, deciduous shrub has burgundy foliage splashed with shades of pink before turning bright red in fall. Shear after flowering or allow to grow into its natural graceful arching shape 4' tall and wide. Zones 4-8

'SILVER MOUND' WORMWOOD
(Artemisia schmidtiana 'Silver Mound')

Who can resist touching this soft, silvery cushion? This could be part of a long-term pairing with the barberry, with the grass being added as an annual in colder areas. Shear lightly in mid-summer to keep foliage at its best. Zones 3-8

RHYTHM 'N BLUES

WHY THIS WORKS

Ribbons of purple and gold weave through this large border, the rhythm being punctuated by mounds of blue oat grass. A large container planted in the combined color palette brings everything into focus. Repetition of just four key plants has been used to create this colorful scene, a design that could easily be scaled down for smaller spaces.

MEET THE PLAYERS

RED LEAF BARBERRY
(Berberis thunbergii 'Atropurpurea')

Great design is based on selecting the right plant for the right place – in this case, the unassuming red leaf barberry. As a 5' fountain it is the perfect color, size and shape to create a backdrop for smaller partners. A deciduous shrub, this barberry turns scarlet in fall. Zones 4-8

BLUE OAT GRASS
(Helictotrichon sempervirens)

In contrast to the fountaining or prostrate forms of its companions, blue oat grass forms tidy, evergreen, 3' hummocks. In spring, gently rake the foliage with your fingers to remove dead blades. This grass is drought tolerant and does well in full sun or part shade. Zones 4-8

VERBENA 'HOMESTEAD PURPLE'
(Verbena canadensis 'Homestead Purple')

Verbena has a sprawling habit that makes 'Homestead Purple' a perfect candidate to mingle with its adjacent partners. Purple flowers cover this woody perennial from spring until fall as it spreads to 3' wide but just 10" high. Zones 7-10

SEDUM 'ANGELINA'
(Sedum rupestre 'Angelina')

This golden evergreen succulent provides a visual frame for all the excitement, seeming to corral the exuberance of the design. In winter, the foliage takes on coppery tints. Drought tolerant and deer resistant. Zones 6-9

RIBBONS AND CURLS

WHY THIS WORKS

Here is a conifer with a serious case of "bad hair day." A wide pink hellebore ribbon tries gallantly to corral those wayward curls, but just when you think it's all under control the broad blades of the pineapple lily get in the way! Funky foliage and unexpected colors make this deer resistant combination both charming and casual.

MEET THE PLAYERS

'GRANNY'S RINGLETS' JAPANESE CEDAR
(Cryptomeria japonica 'Spiralis')

A conifer with attitude! Yellow-green foliage twists in a completely haphazard manner around the stems on this slow growing cultivar. It will eventually reach 20' tall x 10' wide and is hardy in zones 6-10.

MAJORCAN HELLEBORE
(Helleborus lividus)

An unusual hellebore, this species is noted for the overall pink blush and distinctive silver veining on the foliage. In winter, this evergreen perennial blooms with clusters of pink-backed green flowers that persist for several weeks. 1' tall x 2' wide. Zones 7-9

'TUGELA RUBY' PINEAPPLE LILY
(Eucomis comosa 'Tugela Ruby')

Neither a lily nor a pineapple, this herbaceous perennial produces a rosette of green fleshy leaves, heavily flushed with purple. In August, 2'-tall maroon spikes support ivory flowers which resemble elongated pineapples. It grows 2' tall and wide and is hardy in zones 7-9. Do not allow the plant to remain in saturated soil over the winter.

SHIMMER AND SHINE

WHY THIS WORKS

Some plants just beg to be stroked, and this velvety cinquefoil is one of them. Shimmering like a carpet of silver feathers, it easily catches the light and the eye. Partnered with a simple chrysanthemum, it transforms that ordinary perennial into something memorable, and the interplay between the two plants emphasizes the chrysanthemum's pale veins and silvery leaf stalks.

MEET THE PLAYERS

CINQUEFOIL
(Potentilla gelida)

This herbaceous perennial is grown primarily for its foliage and creates a stunning groundcover in sunny areas. The bonus is that in August, deep yellow five-petalled flowers rise above the shining carpet. Grows 12" high and 2' wide. Zones 4-9, possibly colder in a dry climate.

'APRICOT' CHRYSANTHEMUM
(Chrysanthemum 'Apricot')

The deeply-lobed dark green foliage of this herbaceous perennial supports late summer apricot daisies, each with a golden eye. This perennial spreads quickly to form clumps 4' or more in width. Left to its own devices it will reach 4' in height, but is best trimmed back in early summer for a neater shape and greater flower production. Zones 5-9

SIMPLICITY

WHY THIS WORKS

It isn't always about vivacious color combinations – sometimes just green-on-green is all the contrast that is needed for a Nature-inspired design. As the Japanese forest grass and lady's mantle brush the mossy carpet with a soft caress, the slender Hinoki false cypress stands sentry, its splayed foliage a four season living sculpture.

MEET THE PLAYERS

SLENDER HINOKI FALSE CYPRESS
(Chamaecyparis obtusa 'Gracilis')

Layers of dark green fan-like foliage radiate from the trunk of this columnar conifer. Its sculptural profile lends itself to many design aesthetics and at just 15' tall and 6' wide, it is also ideal for small gardens. Happy in full sun or partial shade. Hardy in zones 4-8.

JAPANESE FOREST GRASS
(Hakonechloa macra 'Aureola')

This herbaceous grass will quickly become one of your favorites for the shade garden. Its soft, cascading habit makes it eminently suitable to Asian-inspired design where it blends seamlessly with large, weathered boulders, carpets of moss and sculptural conifers. Hardy in zones 4-9.

LADY'S MANTLE
(Alchemilla mollis)

An enchanting, old-fashioned herbaceous perennial. A tight mound of velvety-soft leaves captures water droplets, which then sparkle like tiny jewels in the sun. Frothy sprays of chartreuse flowers adorn the plants in early summer but should be sheared back when they are past their prime to rejuvenate the plant and reduce self-seeding Happy in full sun or partial shade where it will grow to 18" tall and 2' wide. Zones 2-9

SWEET AND SOUR

WHY THIS WORKS

Just like a great recipe, this combination shares a balance of the sweet, ripe berry tones in the coral bells with the acidic sour of the forest grass and feverfew. The juniper stabilizes the two opposite ingredients with a mild, balancing color of blue that adds another dimension of flavor, effectively breaking the mix into more subtle flavors on the palate.

MEET THE PLAYERS

'BLUE STAR' JUNIPER
(Juniperus squamata 'Blue Star')

This compact, mounding evergreen conifer grows slowly to 3' x 3'. Its unusual icy-blue color makes it a year round winner for containers or the landscape. Zones 4-9

'BERRY SMOOTHIE' CORAL BELLS
(Heuchera 'Berry Smoothie')

One of the most adaptable coral bells, it takes full sun or full shade and copes well with both heat and humidity. In spring, this evergreen perennial is a vibrant raspberry, gradually turning to deeper berry shades as the season progresses. Zones 4-9

GOLDEN FEVERFEW
(Tanacetum parthenium 'Aureum')

Aromatic golden foliage shines the brightest in full sun, but also does well in part shade. In summer, small white daisies add sparkle; these should be deadheaded if you wish to avoid self-seeding. 2' tall and wide. Zones 5-9

'ALL GOLD' JAPANESE FOREST GRASS
(Hakonechloa macra 'All Gold')

A graceful, clumping groundcover with bold chartreuse color, it has the effect of tiny bamboo. Great in part shade/part sun. Ideal for containers or color accent in borders, spreading to 18" tall and wide. Herbaceous. Zones 4-9

TOUGH LOVE

WHY THIS WORKS

These are survivors – ignored by deer, undaunted by neglect and remarkably drought tolerant. Ideal for xeriscaping, this trio will provide year round color and texture. What's not to love?

MEET THE PLAYERS

STONECROP
(Sedum x 'Autumn Joy')

Stonecrop is well known as one of the late summer stars of the garden. These 2' domes of succulent blue-green foliage are topped by clusters of rose-colored flowers that are a butterfly magnet. Cut back this herbaceous perennial by half in early spring to create a more compact plant. Zones 3-10

DAISY BUSH
(Brachyglottis greyi)
(Syn. *Senecio greyi*)

Although this evergreen bush does bloom with yellow daisies in summer, most gardeners grow it for the silvery felted foliage. In a hot, sheltered site this will grow 4' tall and wide, but benefits from being cut back hard in spring to maintain a tidy shape. Zones 7-10

MEXICAN FEATHER GRASS
(Stipa tenuissima)

The soft, billowing mounds of the Mexican feather grass add a wonderful wispy texture that balances the stiffer habit of its partners. This evergreen grass is considered invasive in some states due to self-seeding. Zones 6-10

SITE: Part shade, part sun, full sun	SEASON: Spring-Fall	SOIL: Average	ZONE: 5-7

SHOWY YET SHEER

WHY THIS WORKS

This is a beautiful example of two patterns blending to create one elegant design statement. The same way a skilled clothing designer makes stripes and plaids work together on the runway, this design works in the garden. This duo illustrates two elements: The obvious variegation of white-pink-green in the foliage, and the attention that is drawn to the plants' soft, vertical and horizontal planes. The pale, romantic colors and translucent foliage allow the light to create a sheer effect.

MEET THE PLAYERS

VARIEGATED HEDGE MAPLE
(Acer campestre 'Carnival')

Showy color in the shade is this tree's claim to fame. Slow growing to about 8-10' in ten years. This tree boasts three colors in the early part of the season – pink, cream and green. The pink will fade out to let the white shine in summer. Prefers a fertile, well drained soil. Zones 5-7

VARIEGATED RIBBON GRASS, GARDENER'S GARTERS
(Phalaris arundinacea 'Picta')

Not for the faint of heart, this delicate looking grass is on a mission to take over the world! Consider keeping it corralled in a rhizome barrier or deep pot. Green and white striped blades form dense, spreading clumps from which rise airy panicles of pink seedheads in summer. Cut to the ground in winter. Sun or part shade, average-wet soil. Zones 3-9

STRAWBERRIES AND CHOCOLATE

WHY THIS WORKS

Plants that can go from the ground to a container and back again as the mood or season strikes are always useful to have on hand, even if they do get dizzy in the process! Warm shades of red, cinnamon and bronze are set off by the rich chocolate of this container for a delicious pairing.

MEET THE PLAYERS

'ORANGE ROCKET' BARBERRY
(Berberis thunbergii 'Orange Rocket')

Vibrant shades of rust and orange intensify in fall to give the illusion of a pillar of fire. This new columnar variety of a popular deciduous shrub grows slowly to 4' tall and 18" wide. Zones 4-8

'KALEIDOSCOPE' ABELIA
(Abelia x grandiflora 'Kaleidoscope')

This semi-evergreen shrub has it all: brightly variegated foliage in shades of yellow, green and rosy-red; white flowers for the hummingbirds, and a tidy mounding habit. 2' tall and 3' wide. Zones 6-9

'WINTER CHOCOLATE' HEATHER
(Calluna vulgaris 'Winter Chocolate')

Heather is one of those often-overused plants, yet we chose 'Winter Chocolate' for its colorful foliage. This evergreen perennial transitions through shades of salmon, gold and chocolate, with lavender flowers in late summer. Grows 1' tall and 2' wide. Zones 4-9

STRAWBERRY
(Fragaria × ananassa cultivar)

It's amazing what you can find in the garden to complete a design. The red leaf on this strawberry, together with its ripening fruit, provide the perfect finishing touch – and a delicious treat! Hardiness depends upon cultivar.

A SUMMER DESSERT

WHY THIS WORKS

Who can resist a confection of chocolate, peaches and blueberries? With its silky-smooth chocolate succulent, the cooling touch from the blueberry-hued conifer and the juicy peach coral bells, this recipe has something for everyone. The balance of the three tones creates the perfect interplay with the energetic color of the container. Once the cool fall weather comes, the succulent can be taken inside for protection in cold winter areas and replaced with another sweet ingredient.

MEET THE PLAYERS

'VAN PELT'S BLUE' PORT ORCHARD CEDAR
(Chamaecyparis lawsoniana 'Van Pelt's Blue')

An ideal conifer for containers or as a narrow vertical garden accent, since it grows just 8' x 3' in 10 years. The evergreen powdery-blue foliage is striking year round. For best results, grow in full sun with moisture retentive but well drained soil. Hardy in zones 5-9.

BLACK ROSE
(Aeonium arboreum var. *atropurpureum* 'Zwartkop')

Resembling a chocolate-dipped rose, this glossy succulent is sure to be noticed. Each foliage rosette stands up to 18" high on a sturdy stem. Full sun and well drained soil keep this in top summer condition. Enjoy indoors during colder months. Annual

'PEACH FLAMBÉ' CORAL BELLS
(Heuchera 'Peach Flambé')

THE best coral bells for full sun, it changes color with the season, from flamboyant shades of orange and peach in spring to rich, burnished burgundy in late summer, underpinned year round with tints of raspberry. Sprays of white flowers are an added springtime delight. It will take part shade, but has the best color in full sun. 18" tall and wide. Zones 4-9

| SITE: Full sun | SEASON: Year-round | SOIL: Average, well-drained | ZONE: 6-9 |

SPLASHES AND STRIPES

WHY THIS WORKS

'Magic Carpet' spirea strikes the opening chord with its pink-splashed golden foliage. 'Purple Ruffles' coral bells adds depth, while the spurge brings these colors together and introduces blue-green, which is then repeated by the rue. For this design, another level of artistry comes into play with the details of stems and midribs, while variety in leaf shapes keeps things interesting.

MEET THE PLAYERS

'MAGIC CARPET' SPIREA
(Spiraea japonica 'Magic Carpet')

This wonderful easy-care deciduous shrub forms a tidy 2' mound. New growth is a rich, rosy red, adding drama to the mature golden foliage and hot pink flowers. The colorful display continues in fall as the bush turns vivid red. Zones 4-9

COMMON RUE
(Ruta graveolens)

The feathery blue-green foliage of this 2' tall herbaceous perennial can be used to add a fern-like quality to sunny sites. It needs well drained soil to thrive. Zones 6-11
CAUTION: Skin irritant; wear gloves.

'PURPLE RUFFLES' CORAL BELLS
(Heuchera 'Purple Ruffles')

Growing to 12" tall and wide, this evergreen perennial is at home in containers or gardens. The intense purple leaves have a wonderful frilly edge to set off the white flower spikes that appear in early summer. Beautiful. Zones 4-9

'EXCALIBUR' SPURGE
(Euphorbia 'Excalibur')

Although only a semi-evergreen perennial, it is worthy of year-round status. Red new growth, leaf margins and stems are offset by the olive-green leaves, with a paler midrib and chartreuse bracts in summer. 3' tall and 2' wide. Zones 5-9
CAUTION: Skin irritant. Wear gloves when cutting down older foliage in spring.

shade
COMBINATIONS

BRIGHT LIGHTS, BIG CITY

WHY THIS WORKS

This sophisticated foliage combination is a little bit small town and lot Broadway. The hosta is a traditional and suburban character with tall, upright growth and mellow blue-green color that supports the other actors. The real superstar is the begonia, sporting a cosmopolitan silver and gray-patterned foliage of dramatic, 5-point leaves. Uplighting this show is the bright gold foamy bells that are mingling and having a post-show chat on the lower lever with the similarly-colored volcanic sorrel.

MEET THE PLAYERS

'KROSSA REGAL' HOSTA

(Hosta 'Krossa Regal')

Elegant frosty, blue-green leaves are featured on this vase-shaped perennial. Growing to 40" tall and 3-6' wide, this hardy, slug resistant plant is well loved by hummingbirds for its lavender flowers in summer. Remove dead leaves in winter. Zones 3-9

'GRYPHON' BEGONIA

(Begonia hybrid 'Gryphon')

As a summer annual or houseplant, this begonia is delightful, with large, glossy, silver-splashed leaves. A fast growing plant, it requires little care. Grow it in the shade with a few hours of morning sun at most and it will be 2½' tall and wide. Zones 9-11

'STOPLIGHT' FOAMY BELLS

(Heucherella 'Stoplight')

This traffic-stopping gold foliage is dynamite for its bright glow in the partial shade. The burgundy-red veins make it easy to pair with plants that pick up that tone. Growing 6" tall and 6-10" wide, it has white flowers in late spring. Will be evergreen in mild winter areas.
Zones 4-9

'ZINFANDEL' VOLCANIC SORREL

(Oxalis vulcanicola 'Zinfandel')

A dramatic shamrock: its foliage color is a fantastic backdrop for the gold flowers. Spills beautifully over the edge in summer containers. Prolific growth to 6-12" tall and 12-16" wide. Best in full sun to partial shade as a tender annual, or as a houseplant in winter.
Zones 9-11

DEEP SEA JUNGLE

WHY THIS WORKS

Resembling a giant red squid diving to the bottom of the ocean, the red banana takes center stage in this underwater fantasy. Colorful crotons become a coral reef, while a staghorn fern is transformed into a floating kelp forest in this tropical underworld.

MEET THE PLAYERS

RED BANANA
(Ensete ventricosum 'Maurelii')

Each large, paddle-shaped leaf unfurls from the center of the plant to reveal a blend of red and green, highlighted by a prominent dark midrib. In its native habitat the red banana will reach 30' tall x 15' wide. Keep well watered in full sun or part shade. Zones 9-11

CROTON
(Codiaeum variegatum)

Having waxy, slightly puckered leaves in shades of green, yellow, red and orange, this houseplant makes a colorful, tropical addition to the summer shade garden. To 2' tall and 18" wide. Zones 9b-11

'SULPHUR HEART' PERSIAN IVY
(Hedera colchica 'Sulphur Heart')

Splashed with varying amounts of chartreuse in part shade to full sun, this heart-shaped foliage is deer resistant too. Self-clinging, with a modest growth habit, it is a great alternative to invasive species. Zone 6-9

STAGHORN FERN
(Platycerium bifurcatum)

Staghorn is an evergreen epiphytic fern recognized by its forked foliage, which resembles deer antlers. For a basket display grow in sphagnum moss and do not allow to dry out. To 3' tall and wide. Annual

BRUSHSTROKES

WHY THIS WORKS

Sharing a painterly palette, these shade loving perennials bring an elegant artistry to the garden or container. The soft woodland light makes the fern and coral bells appear luminous, highlighting their broad strokes of silver and hints of burgundy.

MEET THE PLAYERS

JAPANESE PAINTED FERN
(Athyrium niponicum var. pictum)

Surely one of the most beautiful ferns for a woodland glade. The feathery gray-green foliage appears to be brushed with silver, while a delicate line of burgundy highlights the center of each leaf and stem. This herbaceous fern will grow to 18" tall and wide and is hardy in zones 4-9.

'DOLCE BLACKCURRANT' CORAL BELLS
(Heuchera 'Dolce Blackcurrant')

This outstanding evergreen perennial displays shades of silver and burgundy on the surface of its ruffled leaves and raspberry tones underneath. In springtime spires of white flowers bring a fresh look. 2' tall and 1' wide. Zones 4-9

BREAKING BOUNDARIES

WHY THIS WORKS

Blending "indoor" plants with perennial or evergreen foliage is a great way to add a fresh look to combinations. Colorful caladiums, coleus and calathea add excitement to the shades of green offered by the boxwood and the leaves of the golden bleeding heart. (There are six plants in this combination. Two of them, 'Redhead' coleus and 'Goldheart' bleeding heart, are "Supporting Players," shown on page 127.)

MEET THE PLAYERS

'GLENNIS' COLEUS

(Solenostemon scutellarioides 'Glennis')

Glennis is the star of this composition with an exciting display of hot pink, bright green and gold variegated foliage that seems to glow from within. This versatile coleus grows to 24-36" tall in either full sun or full shade. Remove the small blue pineapple-shaped flower spikes as they appear. Annual

DOTTIE' CALATHEA

(Calathea roseopicta 'Dottie')

Intense black, leathery leaves with striking pink markings lend a dramatic tropical punch. A slow growing annual.

'LITTLE GEM' BOXWOOD

(B. microphylla var. *koreana* x *B. sempervirens* 'Green Gem')

This useful evergreen shrub grows as a tidy mound with minimal care. A slow grower to 2' x 2', it is ideally suited to containers and the landscape. Zones 4-9

CALADIUM 'BICOLOR'

(Caladium bicolor)

Large, papery heart-shaped leaves make this an outstanding foliage plant for shade combinations. Cut off older leaves at the base as they discolor. Do not overwater. Annual

DAMP AND DRAMATIC

WHY THIS WORKS

This is all about contrast in shape and size. Pairing the oversized rough foliage of Rodger's flower with the smaller, softer hardy impatiens is genius. Whereas variegated foliage usually takes center stage in a design, here the 'Little Heath' andromeda plays a secondary role by adding sparkle to highlight its companions. This elegant trio flourishes in moist, rich soil.

MEET THE PLAYERS

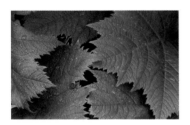

RED LEAF RODGER'S FLOWER
(Rodgersia podophylla 'Rotlaub')

Once seen never forgotten; the giant, jagged leaves of this herbaceous perennial command attention! These heavily textured leaves emerge bronze, slowly creating a 3-4' mound of foliage in shades of green, copper and deep red. These provide a spectacular backdrop for the dramatic plumes of creamy-white flowers in mid-summer. Zones 5-9

HARDY IMPATIENS
(Impatiens omeiana)

Whorls of scalloped, dark green leaves with silvery veins and deep red stalks make an eye-catching addition to the shade border. Creamy-yellow snapdragon-type blooms appear in late summer through fall. This herbaceous perennial spreads slowly to form a tidy clump 18" tall. Zones 6-9

'LITTLE HEATH' LILY OF THE VALLEY SHRUB, ANDROMEDA
(Pieris japonica 'Little Heath')

This compact evergreen shrub deserves a place in every garden. Bright green and white variegated foliage adds sparkle to the shade. Spring sees a flush of red new growth and dangling clusters of bell-shaped white flowers. Slow growing to 3' x 3' , this also works well in containers. Zones 5-9

SUNSET SHADES

WHY THIS WORKS

This color story is woven together using fabric, containers and the foliage plants themselves. Warm sunset tones abound and the graphic cube containers immediately suggest a contemporary design. (There are five plants in this combination. One of them, orange hair sedge, is a "Supporting Player," shown on page 128.)

MEET THE PLAYERS

'ALABAMA SUNSET' COLEUS
(Solenostemon scutellarioides 'Alabama Sunset')

A great foliage accent. Strong, bushy plants will mature at about 2-3' in sun or shade. Leaves are chartreuse tinged with shades of orange and pink. Color will vary depending on the amount of sun it gets. Pinch off blue flowers to maintain shape. Annual

BLACK MONDO GRASS
(Ophiopogon planiscapus 'Nigrescens')

Abuse-proof, drought tolerant, evergreen, good for sun or shade, deer resistant: just a few of the attributes of this striking black grass. Fabulous as a groundcover, accent or container plant. 6" tall and wide. Zones 6-10

PARLOR PALM
(Chamaedorea elegans)

Palms are popular indoor plants that can be used to enliven shady summer plantings. Annual

'SWEET TEA' FOAMY BELLS
(x Heucherella 'Sweet Tea')

Evergreen foliage in shades of cinnamon, copper and burnished orange blend with lighter springtime highlights as the 20" mound of foliage is topped with spikes of fluffy white flowers. Fabulous in full or part shade. Zones 4-9

TWICE LUCKY

WHY THIS WORKS

With each plant displaying a clear pattern of three in its foliage, it is obvious that these two shade lovers have much in common. The shamrock appears at first glance as a miniature version of the trillium in this ephemeral partnership. A delightful woodland-inspired combination.

MEET THE PLAYERS

REDWOOD SORREL, SHAMROCK
(Oxalis oregana)

You may not find the lucky four-leaf clover, but this velvety, evergreen groundcover is delightful anyway. During spring-fall, white flowers with distinct lavender veins stud the carpet of this Northwest native. To 6" high and 2' wide. Zones 7-9

WESTERN TRILLIUM
(Trillium ovatum)

A Northwest native, this charming trillium is a lesson in threes: three-lobed leaves, three sepals and three-petalled flowers are arranged in whorls up a 2' stem. The spring-blooming pristine white flowers age to pink before this perennial fades away altogether in summer. Zones 5-8

| SITE: Part shade | SEASON: Year-round | SOIL: Average, well-drained | ZONE: 6-8 |

A SUCCULENT SPREAD

WHY THIS WORKS

This shallow bedframe is the perfect setting for a slumber party or a pillow fight. The drought tolerant succulents are designed in a sassy patchwork quilt pattern. Lay your head on the soft grasses and look up at the stars. As these colorful gold and burgundy succulents grow and meld together, the planted pattern of plants will create Mother Nature's own coverlet.

MEET THE PLAYERS

HEN AND CHICKS
(Sempervivum tectorum)

These perfect, rubbery rosettes are evergreen. As each mother plant (hen) blooms and dies, the little plantlets (chicks) will quickly fill in. It thrives in dry, rocky soil and full sun, but will also do well with average soil and part shade. Zones 3-11

GOLDEN JAPANESE SEDUM
(Sedum makinoi 'Ogon')

A charming evergreen or semi-evergreen succulent with sunny yellow foliage on pink stems, it spreads slowly to form a mat just 2" high. In hotter climates it prefers some afternoon shade and does well in dry soil. Zones 6-9

BLACK MONDO GRASS
(Ophiopogon planiscapus 'Nigrescens')

This incredibly versatile evergreen grass is happy in full sun or part shade and in either dry or moisture retentive soil. Lilac-colored flowers rise on stems above the deep black blades in summer, followed in fall by black berries. Zones 6-10

SITE: Part shade	SEASON: Year-round	SOIL: Average, well-drained	ZONE: 4-8

21ST CENTURY VOGUE

WHY THIS WORKS

This elegant color combination takes foliage design to a whole new contemporary level. The sophisticated tones of silver, black, chartreuse and cream are both subtle and dramatic at the same time, a signature of the current aesthetic. Add in the patterned foliage layered on top of alternatively very delicate and very broad textured leaves, and you have a feast for the eyes.

MEET THE PLAYERS

GOLDEN BLEEDING HEART
(Dicentra spectabilis 'Gold Heart')

Bright gold, dissected foliage and rose-pink spring flowers make this cultivar a partner that "plays well with others." Its size (24-36" tall and 18-24" wide) makes it easy to snuggle with other plants. In cool zones this plant tolerates more sun; in warmer climates you might give it cooler shade. Zones 3-9

BUGBANE, SNAKEROOT
(Actaea simplex 'Brunette' (syn. *Cimicifuga simplex))*

Chocolate-black tones are fantastic with so many foliage plants. Growing to 3-6' tall and 1-3' wide, it features spikes of fragrant, white flowers that contrast brilliantly with the leaves. A three-season plant, it adds subtle burgundy tones in fall. Zones 4-8

'GHOST' DEAD NETTLE
(Lamium maculatum 'Ghost')

This vigorous silver foliage uplights the part-shade garden with its clusters of magenta flowers. As a mostly evergreen groundcover, it will tolerate dry shade. The leaves shown here have a pink blush, often denoting a virus (which actually adds beauty to the foliage design!). Zones 4-9

'KEY LIME PIE' CORAL BELLS
(Heuchera 'Key Lime Pie')

The showy chartreuse-green foliage is a standout in the part-shade garden. As an evergreen perennial, depending on your climate, it is indispensable to lighten and brighten a dark area. With consistent moisture and drainage, this virtually problem-free plant does beautifully in container combinations, too. Zones 4-9

A HONEY OF A PERSONALITY

WHY THIS WORKS

With Winnie-the-Pooh charm, this hydrangea will quickly win you over. Oozing with personality, it easily makes friends with similarly-colored grasses and draws attention to an unusual fern. Who can resist?

MEET THE PLAYERS

'LITTLE HONEY' HYDRANGEA
(Hydrangea quercifolia 'Little Honey')

A true four season shrub, this hydrangea has large oak leaf-shaped, golden foliage which shines in the shade and sets off the large white cone-shaped summer flowers. In fall, the leaves and stems turn scarlet, often remaining through winter. It grows to a modest 3-4' tall and wide and is hardy in zones 5-9.

HART'S TONGUE FERN
(Asplenium scolopendrium)

An evergreen, glossy fern for the shade garden, its leathery leaves reveal an intricate pattern of cinnamon spores on the undersides. In moist conditions it will grow to 2' tall and wide and is hardy in zones 5-9.

JAPANESE FOREST GRASS
(Hakonechloa macra 'Aureola')

This herbaceous grass forms the most beautiful cascading waterfall of buttery yellow blades, each with a green central stripe. It works well in Asian, woodland or contemporary designs as well as containers. We give it an A+! Hardy in zones 4-9.

WARM AND FUZZY

WHY THIS WORKS

An unusual color partnership and "beg to be touched" textures make this a noteworthy combination. What at first is simply interesting becomes truly fascinating when one's attention is drawn to the color echo between the grass and rust-colored velvet that covers the underside of each Rhododendron leaf – a feature that might otherwise be missed.

MEET THE PLAYERS

RHODODENDRON
(Rhododendron pachysanthum)

Colorful and compact, this evergreen shrub is about far more than just its pretty pale pink flowers. New foliage emerges covered in a soft silver fuzz while the underside of the leaves appear to be covered with a warm cinnamon-colored blanket. 3' tall and wide. Zones 6-8

ORANGE HAIR SEDGE
(Carex testacea)

This is a wonderful evergreen grass whose wispy, olive-green blades are tipped with bronze, a color that intensifies as fall approaches. At 16" tall and 12" wide, it is perfect for containers or the landscape and thrives in sun or partial shade. Zones 7-10

PLUSH VELVET

WHY THIS WORKS

The rich topaz tones of this container nestled in the bed of cool, green groundcover send the eye upward to emphasize the sensuous and velvety colors of this jewel-toned foliage combination. Heart-shaped Siberian bugloss re-enforce the romantic mood, and amethyst-hued bugbane adds a touch of opulence to the sultry scheme. (The fifth member of this group, sweet woodruff, is a "Supporting Player," shown on page 127.)

MEET THE PLAYERS

ROCKET LIGULARIA
(Ligularia stenocephala 'The Rocket')

Dark green toothed foliage remains slug-free in this container – a common problem for in-ground plantings. In summer, tall spikes of yellow flowers appear on purple stems, which provide height – a bonus to the design, though not an essential ingredient. 5' tall and 4' wide. Zones 4-9

'HADSPEN CREAM' SIBERIAN BUGLOSS
(Brunnera macrophylla 'Hadspen Cream')

This is one of the first perennials to appear in spring when it is studded with blue forget-me-not flowers. Wide, irregular creamy yellow margins are the hallmark of this attractive cultivar which grows to 12" x 18" in zones 3-7.

'HILLSIDE BLACK BEAUTY' BUGBANE, SNAKEROOT
(Actaea simplex 'Hillside Black Beauty') (Syn. *Cimifuga simplex)*

Tall 5-7' spires of vanilla-scented white flowers point skyward from the large mass of dramatic chocolate foliage, for a memorable confection. Needs moist shade where it will form a clump 3' wide. Zones 3-8

'CHERRY BERRY' HOSTA
(Hosta 'Cherry Berry')

Delicious and unusual, this green- and white-streaked hosta is noted for its cherry-colored leaf stalks and flower spikes, as well as the seed pods that turn bright red and last through fall. 10" high and 20"wide. Zones 3-8

GOLDEN LIGHTS

WHY THIS WORKS

These partners shine in the shade. Simple repetition of color makes this an easy combination for a container or the garden.

MEET THE PLAYERS

GOLDEN JAPANESE FOREST GRASS
(Hakonechloa macra 'All Gold')

A gentle waterfall of soft yellow, this herbaceous grass thrives in partial shade. 2' tall and wide. Zones 4-9

'MAEJIMA' WINTER DAPHNE
(Daphne odora 'Maejima')

This new introduction is sure to become a favorite. The striking variegated foliage is evergreen and forms a tidy 3' mound. In spring it is adorned with a profusion of light pink, highly fragrant flowers. Zones 7-9

PALM BEACH STYLE

WHY THIS WORKS

What happens when a traditionally preppy color scheme meets tropical plants? You get "Palm Beach," of course! Mixing the elegant leaf pattern of three unique caladiums creates a sense of refinement while the rich colors of the Aglaonema continue the color theme, adding a fresh personality with its stiff, waxy foliage.

MEET THE PLAYERS

'CRETA' AGLAONEMA
(Aglaonema commutatum 'Creta')

Enjoy this tropical perennial in a partial or fully shaded spot outdoors for summer and as a houseplant for the remainder of the year. The thick, leathery leaves are beautifully marked in shades of pink. To 2' tall and wide. Annual

CALADIUM 'BICOLOR'
(Caladium 'Bicolor')

Although there are many named cultivars of caladiums, these three were orphaned! Regardless of lineage, these shade loving plants do well in summer landscapes and containers, providing they are not overwatered. Remove older leaves as they fade. 12" tall and wide. Annual

CALADIUM 'BICOLOR'
(Caladium 'Bicolor')

Although there are many named cultivars of caladiums, these three were orphaned! Regardless of lineage, these shade loving plants do well in summer landscapes and containers, providing they are not overwatered. Remove older leaves as they fade. 12" tall and wide. Annual

CALADIUM 'BICOLOR'
(Caladium 'Bicolor')

Although there are many named cultivars of caladiums, these three were orphaned! Regardless of lineage, these shade loving plants do well in summer landscapes and containers, providing they are not overwatered. Remove older leaves as they fade. 12" tall and wide. Annual

STROKE OF GENIUS

WHY THIS WORKS

Bring the sunshine into the shade garden with this cheerful pair. Splashes of crimson daubed across a canvas of gold create a fun paint box effect, yet the repetition of the yellow tones between the two plants suggests a carefully orchestrated design.

MEET THE PLAYERS

JAPANESE YEW
(Taxus cuspidata 'Dwarf Bright Gold')

This shrubby spreading conifer brings a touch of sunshine to the garden year round with its green and gold variegated needles. It grows slowly to 3-4' tall and wide and is hardy in zones 4-9.

'RED COAT' COLEUS
(Solenostemon scutellarioides 'Red Coat')

One of the most dramatic red coleus, 'Red Coat' has pointed crimson leaves with a wide, irregular gold border. A pretty scalloped edge is also brushed with red. Grows to 2' tall and 18" wide in partial shade or sun. Annual

| SITE: Part shade, part sun | SEASON: Year-round | SOIL: Well-drained | ZONE: 6-9 |

THE SUCCULENT BUFFET

WHY THIS WORKS

It's difficult not to overindulge at the succulent buffet. And since we tend to eat with our eyes, this combination is an enticing dish. The vast range of colors and textures allows for a feast of possibilities in the container or in cracks and crevices in the garden. This photo shows the buffet platter option, laid out with each "dish" neatly arranged. It's OK to mix them up in one space. When they mingle together, the flavors are enhanced. Try them all; you will be back for seconds.

MEET THE PLAYERS

ECHEVERIA
(Echeveria nodulosa)
Dramatic 5"-diameter olive-green rosettes grow in clusters, each parent plant becoming surrounded by smaller offsets. 2' tall flowering stems are thrown up by the central rosette, after which it dies. Prefers partial shade in hotter climates.
Zones 9-11

COPPERTONE, NUSSBAUMER'S SEDUM
(Sedum nussbaumerianum 'Coppertone')
Spills happily over the edge of a container. Fleshy cylindrical foliage turns a vibrant copper shade in the sun, but it is also happy in partial shade. Fragrant pure-white flowers in warm, early spring are a bonus. Grows to 8" tall.
Zones 9-11

HEN AND CHICKS
(Sempervivum tectorum cvs.)
Evergreen and tough, these little succulents are easy to grow and are available in shades of green and dark red. When the central plant blooms and dies, the surrounding plantlets quickly fill in. To 2" tall. Full sun or partial shade. Zones 3-11

GOLDEN JAPANESE SEDUM
(Sedum makinoi 'Ogon')
In hotter areas this low growing sedum prefers afternoon shade where its bright yellow foliage will shine. Semi-evergreen, this spreads slowly to form a dense mat. Zones 6-9

TRIBAL DANCE

WHY THIS WORKS

The aptly named African Mask sets the tempo with its striking arrow-shaped leaves, each one decorated with bold strokes of white. Rex begonia adds a hypnotic quality to the dance with its mesmerizing spirals, while the deep, sultry coleus throbs with a steady beat. Together, this trio creates an unforgettable rhythm.

MEET THE PLAYERS

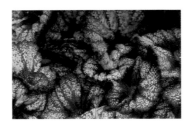

AFRICAN MASK, ELEPHANT EARS
(Alocasia 'Polly')

Although usually grown indoors, this dramatic tropical plant can be used in shade containers outside during summer months. Dark green arrow-shaped leaves accented by clear white veins are held upright on sturdy stems and are so glossy they appear to be polished. Grows slowly to 2' tall and 18" wide. Annual

REX BEGONIA
(Begonia rex)

Rex begonia is a fabulous foliage plant for the home or summer garden with many cultivars available, each with unique markings. Use in the shade garden with finely textured ferns or at the edge of a shady container. Each plant forms a tight clump 12" tall and wide. Be careful not to overwater. Annual

'MERLOT' COLEUS
(Solenostemon scutellarioides 'Merlot')

This adaptable coleus will take sun or shade, growing in an upright fashion to 14" tall and wide. As the rich purple foliage matures, each leaf becomes edged with a delicate green picotee. Annual

LEMON AND LIME

WHY THIS WORKS

The spotted dead nettle can be insignificant as a groundcover, since the color is a rather pale yellow, with a white midrib doing little to add interest. Yet when paired with a variegated weigela, whose foliage is a more elaborate bright green with a double margin of white and yellow, the color echo adds necessary contrast, thereby improving the dead nettle's visibility.

MEET THE PLAYERS

VARIEGATED WEIGELA
(Weigela florida 'Variegata')

This charming old-fashioned shrub has much to offer the gardener. Pretty, variegated foliage adds sparkle to any combination, while the fragrant pink trumpet flowers attract hummingbirds. This deciduous shrub will grow to 6' tall and wide and is happy in full sun or part shade. Zones 4-8

SPOTTED DEAD NETTLE
(Lamium maculatum 'Aureum')

An easygoing groundcover for the shade garden, this creeping perennial is considered evergreen but benefits from shearing after the winter. Heart-shaped pale yellow leaves are decorated with lavender-pink flowers in spring. Part or full shade. Zones 3-8

110

GENTLE TOUCH

WHY THIS WORKS

Like carefully interlaced fingers, the delicate leaves of these two Japanese maples rest gently upon one another, neither asserting dominance over the other, but rather creating a visually pleasing balance of light and dark. The blush on the broader golden leaves echoes its feathery burgundy companion – a comfortable, easy-going partnership.

MEET THE PLAYERS

'AUTUMN MOON' MAPLE
(Acer shirasawanum)

The foliage on this small, upright maple opens burnt orange before turning chartreuse for summer, and finally, a vibrant medley of rich orange and red in fall. It is remarkably heat tolerant and develops the best colors in full sun. Grows 10' tall and wide. Zones 5-9

'CRIMSON QUEEN' JAPANESE MAPLE
(Acer palmatum var. *dissectum* 'Crimson Queen')*

Finely dissected leaves hold their burgundy color all summer, even in full sun, before turning a brilliant scarlet in fall. It forms an attractive mound to 10' tall and 13' wide and is hardy in zones 5-8.

FOUR SEASON KALEIDOSCOPE

WHY THIS WORKS

Take advantage of an expansive view to create an ever-changing scene of colors and textures. Primroses herald spring with fleeting flowers and then with seed heads until late fall. In summer the giant "dinosaur food" plant dominates with monster-sized leaves, while the coral bark maple and sourgum tree become autumn's primary focus. The distant golden western red cedar shines against the winter sky – a striking backdrop. (The cedar is a "Supporting Player," and is shown on page 128.)

MEET THE PLAYERS

CORAL BARK MAPLE
(Acer palmatum 'Sango-kaku')

Brilliant coral-colored bark on younger branches and bright green leaves with red margins that turn a rich golden-yellow in fall: no wonder this is such a popular Japanese maple! A four season star, this grows to 20' tall and wide in full sun or part shade. Zones 5-8

DINOSAUR FOOD
(Gunnera manicata)

Resembling giant rhubarb, this fast growing herbaceous perennial knows how to make a statement! Each enormous, puckered leaf can measure several feet across, with the clump easily reaching 8' x 8'. It needs constant moisture and in colder areas it is necessary to protect the crown in winter. Zones 6-8

CANDELABRA PRIMULA
(Primula bulleyana)

Although primarily grown for its sunny springtime flowers, this herbaceous perennial offers great texture with its tiers of globular seed heads. Planted en masse, they form a striking counterpoint to larger foliage. 2' tall and wide. Zones 4-9

SOURGUM TREE
(Nyssa sylvatica)

Great for a muddy spot, the sourgum is a favorite for its fall color. A psychedelic display of yellow, orange, red and purple makes this a standout in full sun or partial shade. 30-50' tall and 20-30' wide. Zones 4-9

HOSTA HIGHLIGHTS

WHY THIS WORKS

Pairing two hostas that display "reverse variegation" can be a fun way to add some spice to the shade garden. Blue and chartreuse trade places in the foliage of these two cultivars.

MEET THE PLAYERS

'GOLD STANDARD' HOSTA
(Hosta 'Gold standard')

Once seen, never forgotten. A mature specimen can be 5' across and 2' tall, shining like a pot of gold and visible from a considerable distance. Each large, golden leaf is accented by a blue margin – stunning. In mid-summer, pale lavender flowers are held high above the foliage. Bait for slugs. Zones 4-8

'TOKUDAMA FLAVOCIRCINALIS' HOSTA
(Hosta 'Tokudama Flavocircinalis')

Thick, rounded, corrugated blue leaves are accented by a wide gold margin, making it an exciting companion for 'Gold Standard'. This cultivar grows more slowly to 4' wide and 18" tall. Zones 4-8

SITE: Part shade, part sun	SEASON: Year-round	SOIL: Average, moisture retentive	ZONE: 7

FOLIAGE FUSION

WHY THIS WORKS

'Goldcrest' Monterey cypress sets a bright chartreuse note in this container design. 'Sunrise' abelia introduces red tones, which are then repeated in the foliage of both the fringe flower and fuchsia. The bright green leaves of the foam flower keep things fresh, while the bronze sweet potato vine adds a softness to the overall scheme. The fringe flower and sweet potato vine are "Supporting Players," shown on page 128.

MEET THE PLAYERS

'GOLDCREST' MONTEREY CYPRESS

(Cupressus macrocarpa 'Wilma Goldcrest')

A lemon scent and bright chartreuse foliage make this columnar conifer a favorite for containers and landscapes. Slow growing to 6-8' tall and 2' wide. Zones 7-10

GARTENMEISTER FUCHSIA

(Fuchsia triphylla 'Gartenmeister Bonstedt')

This upright-growing fuchsia is happy in sun or partial shade, offering tubular brick-red flowers for the hummingbirds and rich bronze foliage for the designer. Dead heading not necessary. 3' tall and 2' wide. Zones 9-11 or annual

'SUNRISE' ABELIA

(Abelia x grandiflora 'Sunrise')

Variegated semi-evergreen foliage and fragrant summer flowers make this a useful shrub that is also popular with hummingbirds and butterflies. To 4' tall and wide. Zones 6-9

'SILVERADO' FOAM FLOWER

(Tiarella wherryi 'Silverado')

This compact, evergreen perennial thrives in partial or full shade. Fresh green foliage is topped with frothy white flower spikes in spring that can be trimmed off when they fade. 12" tall and wide. Zones 4-7

DOWN THE RABBIT HOLE

WHY THIS WORKS

Piercing through the groundcover, this perfectly formed but diminutive Japanese maple appears to be hovering over a meadow, creating an Alice in Wonderland effect as we "giants" tower overhead. Delightful contrasts in color and texture make this a striking duo.

MEET THE PLAYERS

'KAMAGATA' JAPANESE MAPLE
(Acer palmatum 'Kamagata')

This dwarf Japanese maple may look delicate, but it does well even in full sun and dry soil. Slow growing to 3-4', it forms a dense, rounded bush with striking fall color in shades of gold and orange brushed with red. Zones 5-9

STONECROP
(Sedum hybridum 'Immergrunchen')

Forming a dense mat of succulent green foliage for most of the year, this sedum sprouts 6" spikes of yellow summer flowers, which add to the "meadow" effect. Drought tolerant and deer resistant, this groundcover is tough, versatile and low maintenance. Zones 4-9

SITE: Part shade, part sun	SEASON: Year-round	SOIL: Average	ZONE: 4-8

JEWEL BOX

WHY THIS WORKS

Like precious stones sparkling in the sun, these annuals reflect the light in a dazzling display even in a partially shaded container. The evergreen golden conifer lends a sense of solidity to these frivolous annuals, yet is equally brilliant in its own right.

MEET THE PLAYERS

'GAY'S DELIGHT' COLEUS
(Solenostemon scutellarioides 'Gay's Delight')

A fabulous contemporary color blend of bright chartreuse foliage etched with black veins. Stunning in moderate sun or partial shade, this grows to 3' tall and 18" wide. Annual

PERSIAN SHIELD
(Strobilanthes dyerianus)

With its iridescent foliage in shades of purple, green and silver, this is both unusual and eye-catching. Let it meander among its neighbors for unexpected combinations! To 3' tall and 2' wide. Annual

'FRECKLES' COLEUS
(Solenostemon scutellarioides 'Freckles')

Leaves splashed in shades of bronze and orange on a lemon base make this an exciting cultivar. To 3' tall and 18" wide. Pinch off growing tips occasionally to keep it bushy. Annual

GOLDEN HINOKI CYPRESS
(Chamaecyparis obtusa 'Fernspray Gold')

This is a wonderful sculptural conifer with golden fern-like foliage that takes on an orange cast in winter. Slow growing to 10' tall and 5' wide. Zones 4-8

HOLIDAY BLING!

WHY THIS WORKS

Add a little seasonal flair to your containers! The interesting and colorful foliage of the holly and grasses forms the "bones" of this design, which can quickly be dressed up with holiday ornaments, sprigs of evergreens cut from the garden and berried stems. Tip: Don't use "everlasting" berry ornaments in exposed areas. After a heavy rain it will resemble a murder scene (speaking from experience here!).

MEET THE PLAYERS

'GOLD COAST' ENGLISH HOLLY
(Ilex aquifolium 'Gold Coast')

Clean, yellow variegation and glossy foliage are the hallmarks of this holly. This male form is not invasive but will pollinate other nearby female English hollies. Slow growing to 4-6' tall and wide, but can be kept smaller with trimming. Zones 6-9

LEATHERLEAF SEDGE
(Carex buchananii)

Wispy blades in warm shades of brown offer year round interest. Growing to 3' tall and wide, it is drought tolerant but does better with regular water. Zones 6-9

BLACK MONDO GRASS
(Ophiopogon planiscapus 'Nigrescens')

A fabulous "ever-black" perennial for sun or shade, wet or dry. Lilac-colored summer flowers are followed by black berries. A standout for gardens and containers. Zones 6-10

SUPPORTING PLAYERS

Each plant on these pages is a star in its own right, and we love them all. But within the foliage combinations they belong to, each plays a supporting role only. We don't want you to miss seeing their beautiful faces up close, so here are our "supporting players."

A MAGICAL JOURNEY

'GOLDEN SPIRIT' SMOKE BUSH
(*Cotinus coggygria* 'Golden Spirit')
Zones 4-8
(see page 18)

EMPRESS TREE
Paulownia tomentosa
Zones 5-9
(see page 18)

BLACK MONDO GRASS
(*Ophiopogon planiscapus* 'Nigrescens')
Zones 6-10
(see page 18)

BALANCING ACT

'TRICOLOR' NEW ZEALAND FLAX
(*Phormium cookianum* 'Tricolor')
Zones 7-11
(see page 8)

BLUES ON FIRE

BLUE SWITCHGRASS
(*Panicum virgatum* 'Heavy Metal')
Zones 4-9
(see page 22)

DEER BE DAMNED

'BLACK LACE' ELDERBERRY
(*Sambucus nigra* 'Black Lace')
Zones 4-7
(see page 10)

QUIET ELEGANCE

'OCTOBER DAPHNE' STONECROP
(*Sedum sieboldii*)
Zones 3-9
(see page 44)

GRACEFUL GRASSES

BLUE FESCUE
(*Festuca glauca*)
Zones 3-9
(see page 34)

SUPPORTING PLAYERS

IN THE LIMELIGHT

PLUSH VELVET

STONECROP
(Sedum spectabile 'Neon')
Zones 3-9
(see page 28)

'OCTOBER DAPHNE'
STONECROP
(Sedum sieboldii)
Zones 3-8
(see page 28)

NEW ZEALAND WIRE
NETTING BUSH
(Corokia cotoneaster
'Little Prince')
Zones 7-11
(see page 28)

SWEET WOODRUFF
(Gallium odorata)
Zones 5-9
(see page 98)

STRAWBERRIES AND CHOCOLATE

BREAKING BOUNDARIES

'SIROCCO'
PHEASANT TAILS
GRASS
(Stipa arundinacea
'Sirocco')
Zones 4-9
(see page 68)

'SWEET TEA' FOAMY
BELLS
(x *Heucherella*
'Sweet Tea')
Zones 4-9
(see page 68)

'GOLDHEART'
BLEEDING HEART
(Dicentra spectabilis
'Goldheart')
Zones 3-9
(see page 82)

'REDHEAD' COLEUS
Solenostemon hybrida
'Redhead')
Annual
(see page 82)

SUPPORTING PLAYERS

FOLIAGE FUSION		FOUR SEASON KALEIDOSCOPE	SUNSET SHADES

'RAZZLEBERRI' FRINGE FLOWER
(Loropetalum chinense 'Razzleberri')
Zones 7-10
(see page 118)

'SWEET CAROLINE' BRONZE SWEET POTATO VINE
(Ipomoea batatas)
Annual
(see page 118)

GOLDEN WESTERN RED CEDAR
(Thuja plicata 'Aurea')
Zones 5-9
(see page 114)

ORANGE HAIR SEDGE
(Carex testacea)
Zones 6-9
(see page 86)

Index

* These plants may be invasive in some areas.
Please consult your local Cooperative Extension
or County Extension Office.

Note: Although we have listed several plants as
'deer resistant' it should be understood that this
depends upon regional taste, hunger and sheer
deer inquisitiveness.

Foliage Combinations

Trademarked and Registered Plants

The following plants are either trademarked or registered by the owners shown below. If we have not acknowledged other plants that belong on this list, we apologize for the inadvertent omission.

Proven Winners
Little Henry® dwarf Virginia sweetspire; Little Henry® *Itea virginica*
My Monet® weigela; My Monet® *Weigela florida*
Dolce® Blackcurrant coral bells; Dolce® Blackcurrant *Heuchera*
Dolce® Key Lime Pie coral bells; Dolce® Key Lime Pie *Heuchera*
Zinfandel™ volcanic sorrel; Zinfandel™ *Oxalis vulcanicola*
Black Lace™ Elderberry; Black Lace™ *Sambucus nigra*

Monrovia Nursery, Inc.
Gold Coast® English Holly; *Ilex aquifolium* 'Monvila'
Razzleberri® Fringe Flower; Razzleberri® *Loropetalum chinense*
Bountiful Blue® Blueberry; Bountiful Blue® *Vaccinium corymbosum*

Anthony Tesselaar, Inc.
Canna Tropicanna®

Acknowledgments

from both of us

~

We naively thought just the two of us were writing this book. In fact it has taken a team of courageous and generous people to make it all happen – and a lot of chocolate. Perhaps the bravest of them all was our publisher, Paul Kelly, who took a gamble with two first time authors – thank you for believing in us. A sense of humor is critical to surviving such a project and thankfully our "dream editor," Cathy Dees, has that in abundance. She is also now officially bilingual and can translate between American English and the Queen's English with ease – usually.

Then there are those who make us look really good! Photography is an art form and our wonderful photographer, Ashley DeLatour, is a true artist. Her patience, dedication and commitment to *Fine Foliage* have made this book what we envisioned. Asking Ashley to stand in bushes and contort herself into positions to get just the right shot was sometimes necessary, and she rose to the occasion with aplomb. Art director Holly Rosborough took our ideas and brought them to life, far surpassing our expectations – thank you.

We especially wish to acknowledge the following who opened their gardens and nurseries to us, often at anti-social hours and also those who generously shared their expertise: Larry and Connie Adams, Jim Guthrie, Carol Johanson, Peggy and Al Shelley, Joanne White, Alyson and Mike Markley, Brian Coleman, Judy Massong, Ron Allesandrini and Mike Osterling, Molbak's Garden + Home, Boxhill Farm and Nursery, T and L Nursery, JB Instant Lawn, Newcastle Fruit and Produce, Duvall Nursery, Bellevue Botanical Gardens, RHR Horticulture, Glenn Withey, Charles Price, and Debra Lee Baldwin. A special thank you also to Debra Prinzing, who introduced us to St. Lynn's Press, cheered us along the way and graciously wrote the back cover review.

from Karen

To my amazing daughter, Katie, who has helped me with everything from punctuation to photography and to my son, Paul, who gave up asking what was for dinner and just started cooking – thank you. Finally, my greatest thanks and love to my ever patient husband, Andy, whose 24/7 tech support, steady supply of wine and chocolate and encouraging words have made it possible for me to follow my dreams.

from Christina

I am ever grateful for the support of my dear friend Heather Bradley. She gave me encouragement, inspiration and played a crucial role in late night texting of my plant name questions – and the greatest laughs. My daughter, Tasha, was instrumental in providing two exceedingly important things: candy and back massages. However, the most love and gratitude I owe to my husband, David. He is my tech support guru, provider of appropriate ooohs and ahhhs over my work, and best promoter ever.

About the Authors

Karen Chapman is proprietor of Le Jardinet, a custom container and landscape design business in the Seattle area. She writes regular garden-related articles for online and print publications and her work has been featured in numerous national magazines, including *Fine Gardening* and *Decks, Patios and Pools*. Karen is also a popular speaker at garden clubs, nurseries and the annual Northwest Flower and Garden Show.

She lives on five rural acres in Duvall, Washington, where she is trying to create her dream garden – despite the deer. Website and blog: www.lejardinetdesigns.com

"There has been a trowel in my hand and soil under my fingernails for as long as I can remember, but that is just the way it is in England where I grew up. Gardening is simply a part of everyday life where plants and produce are exchanged over a cup of tea and neighbors regularly stop to admire one another's gardens. And so it was inevitable that when I moved to the Pacific Northwest in 1996 it wasn't long before I was working at one of the leading nurseries, where I could continue to feed my plant addiction and share my enthusiasm and knowledge with others. Ten years later I took that a step further by establishing my custom container garden and landscape design business, Le Jardinet."

Christina Salwitz is a horticulturist with a passion for great design and all things green and beautiful. Her Seattle-area business, The Personal Garden Coach, helps gardeners of all skill levels to achieve their gardening dreams with style and originality. Christina's "couture" plants, custom designed containers and writing have been featured in *Better Homes & Gardens* and *Fine Gardening*, among others, and she is a regular speaker at garden shows and nurseries.

She feeds her foliage obsession in her Renton, Washington, garden – determined to cram as many luscious leaves as possible into a small space.
Blog: www.personalgardencoach.wordpress.com

"Early in life, I was going to be in Fashion and Merchandising, never dreaming that it would one day take me into couture plants and container plant displays instead. After being an avid gardener all my life, it finally became clear what I truly wanted to be when I grew up. After working in nurseries for many years, becoming a horticulturist and designer, I started The Personal Garden Coach. Now I happily guide other gardeners through the challenges and pleasures of gardening practice and design. With the temperate climate in the Northwest, we're blessed to be able to garden almost year-round. I focus on container design as my main passion, but my signature style is to blend fabulous foliage while paying special attention to brightening the gray months of winter."

About the Photographer

A graduate of the Art Institute of Seattle, **Ashley DeLatour** is a fine art/ people/garden/travel photographer, and co-owner of One Thousand Words Photography in Seattle. Her journey into garden photography began with Karen Chapman showing her the world of plant combinations and the beauty and details that lie within a garden. Ashley's work has been featured in *Fine Gardening, Seattle Bride,* and *The Knot* magazines; and on the blog "Garden Adventures – for thumbs of all colors."

She is co-author of the blog: http://onethousandwordsaminute.com/

Photo Credits

All images taken by **Ashley DeLatour**, except for the following:

Karen Chapman (Foliage Fusion, Golden Lights, Harmony, Holiday Bling, Warm and Fuzzy, Graceful Grasses, Deep Sea Jungle, Jewel Box, Stroke of Genius, Brush Strokes)

Christina Salwitz (Three-Leaf Trifecta , Double Duty Design, Rich and Regal)

Design and Location Credits

Design

Karen Chapman (Foliage Fusion, Holiday Bling, Palm Beach Style, Tribal Dance, Blues On Fire!, Deer Be Damned, Lethal Beauty, Strawberries and Chocolate, Brush Strokes, and Design, Divide, Repeat)

Christina Salwitz (21st Century Vogue, Bright Lights Big City, A Three-Leaf Trifecta, In The Limelight, Leaf Pattern Paradigm, Breaking Boundaries, Sweet and Sour, Balancing Act, Double Duty Design, Rich and Regal, Splashes and Stripes)

RHR Horticulture http://rhrhorticulture.com/ (Deep Sea Jungle, Stroke of Genius, Jewel Box)

Locations

Connie and Larry Adams (Damp and Dramatic, Hosta Highlights, Lethal Beauty)

Ron Allesandrini and Mike Osterling (Plush Velvet)

Bellevue Botanical Gardens (Golden Lights, Luscious Layers, Twice Lucky, Curtain Call, Easy on the Eyes, Graceful Grasses, Shimmer and Shine, Tough Love)

Brian Coleman (Deep Sea Jungle, Jewel Box, Stroke of Genius)

Jim Guthrie (Harmony)

Carol Johanson (Purple Waves)

Alyson and Mike Markley (Honey of a Personality, Sunset Shades, Simplicity, A Magical Journey)

Judy Massong (Warm and Fuzzy)

Peggy and Al Shelley (Lemon and Lime, Quiet Elegance, Fatal Attraction, Rhythm 'n Blues)

Joanne White (A Succulent Spread, Berry-licious, Down the Rabbit Hole, Four Season Kaleidoscope, The Succulent Buffet, A Summer Dessert, A Thug, a Bully and a Gentle Giant, All That Glitters, Masterpiece, Ribbons and Curls, Showy Yet Sheer)